Were You There?

By arrangement with BBC Enterprises Limited
and the BBC's Religious Programmes Department

Were You There?

Surviving Life's Setbacks

Rosemary Hartill

First published 1995
SPCK
Holy Trinity Church Marylebone Road
London NW1 4DU

British Library Cataloguing in Publication Data

A catalogue record for this book is available from the
British Library.

ISBN 0-281-04834-7

Typeset by PDQ Repro Ltd, Bungay, Suffolk

Printed in Great Britain by
Cromwell Press, Melksham, Wilts

Contents

Introduction

1	Loneliness	5
2	Fear	27
3	Anger	49
4	Disappointment	77
5	Stress	99
6	Guilt	123

Acknowledgements 143

Further Reading 145

In affectionate memory
of
Gerald Priestland

Introduction

The Sufi Bayazid says this about himself:
I was a revolutionary when I was young and all my prayer to God was: 'Lord, give me the energy to change the world.'

As I approached middle age and realized that half my life had gone without my changing a single soul, I changed my prayer to: 'Lord, give me the grace to change all those who come in contact with me. Just my family and friends, and I shall be content.'

Now that I am an old man, and my days are numbered, my one prayer is, 'Lord, give me the grace to change myself.' If I had prayed for this right from the start, I should not have wasted my life.

(from Song of the Bird, *Anthony de Mello)*

That story is at the very heart of this book; for the Moslem Sufi did not say it was impossible to change the world; he said he had first to change himself.

Traditional religion—whether Islamic, Jewish, Christian or almost any other—speaks in glowing images of peace, togetherness, calm, love, light. Yet everyone has experiences of the reverse—of loneliness, disappointment, anger, violence, stress, and guilt.

Yet how can we move from anger to calm, from hate to love, from stress to peace? Are black times inevitable for all of us at some time? Does any knowledge emerge from that experience that can be used for the better later on?

To try and tap into the vast well of lived experience, the BBC's

Religious Programmes Department asked Radio 4 listeners to write or phone in with their stories, and to describe what had helped them. Hundreds of letters began arriving, and out of those honest and often moving experiences, a series of six 45-minute radio programmes grew, which I presented. They were broadcast on Radio 4 on Sunday mornings, during the six weeks of Lent 1994—a radical departure for Radio 4 scheduling, which normally broadcasts church-based worship at this hour on Sundays.

With the letters as a core, together with some readings and music from many different sources around the world, we asked two or three guests to take part in each programme; people whose lives had been profoundly affected by the emotion concerned. All had not only experienced something very deep and at times painful, they had also tried to face the truth about themselves and their situation honestly; they had a spiritual dimension to their lives, and had transformed what had happened into something positive and creative. They were also willing to risk the vulnerability of sharing that journey with others.

Each programme included a passage from the Passion story and ended with a meditation with prayers and music, reflecting on what had been heard.

Each week nearly one and a half million people tuned in, and soon hundreds and hundreds more letters began to arrive. 'How dare you take over the morning service slot,' wrote one furious listener. 'What arrogance, as if you have something better to offer!' Atheists joined in too: 'Who is responsible for the latest load of crap? Religion, like politics is an on-going leper scourge. God is a man-made invention.'

But the huge majority of letters were from enthusiastic listeners: 'In all the many years of listening to Radio 4, I cannot remember one I have appreciated more,' wrote one listener. Another said the series had been the most powerful religious experience she had ever had.

A non-Christian sent this:

Time was, I use to run for the off-switch, soon as Alistair Cooke finished, before the service came on. . .

But recently, I was a bit slow getting to the button, and this wonderful human stuff came on. This is religion? How come it talks about real things? I'm not used to this. It's enough to turn me on to God. Almost.

Our aim was to try and be honest, and be alongside listeners, in conversation with anyone with a spiritual dimension to their lives, however alienated from the traditional churches. In preparing this book, I have tried to do the same, reorganising and recasting a little, and also adding a handful of extra readings and letters, which were squeezed out from the series for reasons of time. I have included details of music used in the programmes, and biographical material about each guest opens each chapter.

I learned much from the experiences people shared. The many who risked telling those stories, in the hope that something good would come out of them, are the real authors of this book, not me. To all of them, thank you.

Rosemary Hartill
Northumberland, 21 August 1994

SISTER WENDY BECKETT is a contemplative nun who lives in solitude in the grounds of a monastery in Norfolk. Educated at Oxford University, where she took a Congratulatory First in English, she has since gained an international reputation as an art expert and critic, writing regularly on fine art for specialist magazines, and for the national press, as well as presenting BBC television series about art—Sister Wendy's Odyssey, and Sister Wendy's Grand Tour. She has advised on selections for exhibitions in Britain, Russia and the USA.

ROSEMARY WAKELIN is a Methodist minister, currently working in Norwich. For seven years, she lived in Africa, the wife of a missionary doctor in Sierra Leone and Kenya. In the first year of their marriage, her husband Paul was treated for tuberculosis in a sanatorium; later she herself contracted amoebic hepatitis. Now a widow, with three grown-up children, she enjoys freelance writing and broadcasting.

ONE

Loneliness

I am alone. I have no job. I live entirely on benefits, and I am finding it hard at 46 to start all over within the community.

When the children have gone to school and my husband to work, the day stretches out like a vast, empty desert. It's the loneliness that wears me down the most.

(Perth)

My partner committed suicide eighteen months ago. I haven't found very many people I can talk to, because we were living irregularly as it were, and I was really only the other woman.

I am gay. My partner and I did everything together, saw everyone together, slept together, and when he died, I found myself so utterly alone.

(Newton Abbot)

I'm a nineteen-year-old boy, and being shy, and not very outgoing, I predictably seem to spend a lot of time on my own, dwelling on the constant feelings of loneliness. Many people must have asked themselves like me, 'Why does nothing stay the same? Where did I go wrong?'

(Manchester)

God has let me down. He said, 'I will never leave you or forsake you', but he has me. No one cares about me.

(Merthyr Tydfil, woman)

In 1913, the young poet, Rupert Brooke, sailed to America from Liverpool docks. Everyone else seemed to have friends; he had none. Eventually, looking down from the liner, he saw on the quay a scruffy little boy. He discovered his name was William. 'Will you wave to me if I give you sixpence, William?' 'Why yes,' said William. So back to the ship went the poet. And when the vast liner slipped away, and friends and family waved to friends and family, a dirty rag was waved by a dirty hand. 'So,' wrote the poet later, 'I got my sixpennorth and my farewell—dear William!'

Anyone who has ever felt lonely knows isolation has little to do with how many people are around. Rupert Brooke admitted his loneliness; but in other circumstances, many of us are reluctant to do so—seeing it a sign of failure, rather than something which most people experience at one time or another. Isolation may be inevitable at some point in our lives. If so, does it help to accept that? If we feel abandoned, are we sure we are not also abandoning others? And since some can spend a lifetime almost totally alone, yet in almost perfect happiness, how can others move from the misery of loneliness to this happier state of solitude?

It was during the early part of her married life, a period when few people would expect loneliness, that Rosemary Wakelin came sharply face to face with it. She was living in Africa—in Sierra Leone and Kenya—with her doctor husband:

> There were bits that were happy, but an awful lot of it was not, no. I believed I was doing the right thing, and I suppose there's a sort of happiness there, but quite a lot of it was very lonely. My husband was working all the hours there were, and I didn't see him very often, and I did feel isolated and alone.

Sister Wendy Beckett, on the other hand, has for years deliberately chosen solitude. A contemplative nun, dressed in her habit of black and white, she has lived alone for 24 years in a caravan, deep in rural Norfolk. To make her BBC television programmes, *Sister Wendy's Odyssey* and *Sister Wendy's Grand Tour*, she travelled to great cities like Madrid and Venice to talk about some of the finest paintings in the world; yet she was never tempted to give up her solitary life in the caravan:

> What I was tempted to do was to give up the television series! There's no doubt in my mind that there's no greater

joy than to live in solitude. Remember, that is not loneliness. Loneliness is a state of unhappiness, and nearly always it's been foisted on you, you haven't chosen it. Whereas solitude may start by being foisted on you, but normally it's a choice, a rare choice, and it's a life of complete happiness.

The letters and calls we received focused mostly on stories of long-term loneliness, loneliness through illness and loneliness through bereavement.

1 Loneliness through Bereavement

Ash Wednesday lunchtime 1993. I am recently retired at 76 after a lifetime of business. Pam, my partner, aged 50, is a solicitor's secretary, happy in her work. We enjoyed our pastie and treacle tart, and laughed over the usual debate about what we should give up for Lent. She returned to work and was calling on a sick friend to cheer her up on her way home. Pam cheered her friend up, but on reaching the car to return home fell backwards dead. What do I give up this year?

(Teignmouth, Devon)

In September 1974, I lost my husband suddenly as he had a brain haemorrhage ... The days seemed an eternity and I had to set myself small tasks to get through the moments. Each weekend I went to the New Forest and walked miles ... During the week I helped my mother in law with shopping, washing etc. All the time I felt a gnawing inside and a longing to scream.

(Newbury)

I find the mornings worst of all, to wake on your own is difficult and to face each day with no one to look out for and care about. Everything seems meaningless. People say, 'Oh, time is a great healer', but how can they know the emptiness and despair one feels, until they've been touched themselves.

(Newton Abbot, man)

When Rosemary Wakelin's husband died fifteen years ago, she

had not realised how much like physical pain bereavement is:

> You hurt terribly. They were building a new road out to Yarmouth, and I remember seeing two beautiful trees that had grown together, and made a pattern in the sky. They cut one down, and I just couldn't believe it, because I love trees, and the other tree was left, and I thought, 'That feels like me'. One side was lovely, but the side that had related to the other tree was torn and bruised and ragged, and that was just how I felt, and I was hurting and bleeding inside, terrible emptiness and pain.

The second letter-writer above, who when grieving walked miles in the New Forest, met another partner three years after her husband's sudden death; she expects to remain with him for life. Yet, as the third letter-writer commented, being told that time will heal feels absolutely of no help at the beginning—a view shared by Rosemary Wakelin:

> People, very righteous, pious people say God should be enough, but in fact you find yourself banging at God and asking for help. There's a lovely bit in the book *A Grief Observed* by C. S. Lewis, where he describes the death of his wife, and how afterwards he felt as if he were banging against God's door; and all he could hear were the bolts and bars being more firmly shut against him. But he experienced, and I have to say that I did too, that he was (to change the metaphor!) barking up the wrong tree. God was actually on the same side of the door as he was. When you stop making so much noise and thrashing around, you find that God is with you all the time; but you don't always realise that until later, when you look back.

Talking about her husband was, and still is, a great help:

> One of the problems when you are bereaved is that you are isolated, because people are frightened of talking to you. I'm sure it's from the sweetest motives. They don't want to intrude on your grief; they don't want to tread where perhaps they feel you're hurting; and they may also be frightened you're going to cry all over them, or something like that, and so they pull back. Actually you want them to talk to you.

Rosemary was teaching at the time; she found the children hugely comforting, because they were not afraid to break that invisible barrier:

> One dear little boy, whom my husband had known quite well, said, 'Your husband died because his heart attacked him.' It was such a glorious remark. That was the first time I laughed after he died.

The Jews have a tradition of a highly formalised period of mourning. For a period of seven days, friends and relations come to the house to sit with the close relatives. This allows time to recall together all the good memories, as well as to express their grief and loneliness and regrets. Of course, visitors chat among themselves too—part of an outside world, which is continuing to live its life, however much the bereaved feel that life has lost all meaning and purpose. Jews feel that helps keep death in perspective; but they also consider it takes a year to get over a close death.

One Bristol listener described how it took sixteen years after the death of her mother, before she let out her bottled-up grief:

> I'm now 40, my mother died when I was twenty. It wasn't until about four years ago that I noticed I'd been burying the grief for her and it had never really come out. There was nobody I could really talk to, and I went to see the local curate, and said things like 'There's a black hole inside me'; and he said, 'Well, try and let go'. And I said I was afraid to let go of it, because it was me. And he said, 'God would fill the hole'. There were floods of tears and I came back and thought about what he said, and experienced a great letting go that evening. Of course he was right—the black hole was no longer there. A feeling of warmth came into my heart, and after a couple of weeks I felt like it was my birthday and I was on cloud nine. I still get moments of great intensity where I feel God's Love.'

Rosemary Wakelin was reminded by this letter of Dietrich Bonhoeffer, the German pastor and theologian who was arrested by the Nazis, separated from his family and fiancée, and eventually executed in a prison camp:

He wrote, in a sense rather differently to what she's saying, that God actually doesn't fill the hole, he allows it to remain as the place of memory. So although, in a way, you heal, the scar stays; and that's part of the blessing of memory. You let go, in that you let someone die, but you also retain that love, and that precious part of the relationship; and that's important, too. You do heal, and the violent rough pain becomes a dull ache, but that space which was occupied in my case by my husband, can never be filled by anybody else. It's also a precious place, because that's where I keep my memory of him, and am aware of his love.

A number of bereaved listeners found festivals like Christmas or birthdays particularly difficult. One West Midlands listener had cared for many years for her mother. These extracts came from her diary during the months after her mother's death:

Christmas is drawing nearer every day. The usual Christmas tasks I perform on mother's behalf, then remember she is no longer with us. Depression takes over most of the time. Is the Christmas story really true? ... I listen to the news on my radio which convinces me that God is non-existent. Please, please, will someone help me carry this burden for it gets heavier.

Five months later, this everlasting loneliness is very frightening. I am told people's grief may last twelve months or even longer and may take various forms ...

Six months later, she had overcome her depths of bitterness and despair. After praying at her mother's grave, she experienced a real sense of peace and comfort:

I can hear the birds—the time of the singing of the birds is here. From the grief of the grave, today my stone is rolled away and my joy knows no bounds.

That listener found herself using imagery from the story of Christ's crucifixion and resurrection; nearly every crucifixion picture includes a portrait of Christ's friends grieving at the foot of the cross:

A number of women were also present, watching from a distance. Among them were Mary of Magdala, Mary the mother of James the younger and of Joseph, and Salome, who had all followed him and waited on him when he was in Galilee, and there were several others who had come up to Jerusalem with him.

Mark 15.40–41 (NEB)

To Sister Wendy, the greatest painter of the crucifixion is Grunewald, because he shows the reality of suffering:

Everybody in the reproduction of the painting I have before me now is truly in agony. People so easily tend to say, 'If you love God enough, of course you won't feel it so much.' And of course this is just nonsense. The dead Jesus here was ravaged by pain, and round the cross stand the three who loved him most, Mary his mother, Mary Magdalen and John.

What she finds so moving about this particular Grunewald, the small crucifixion, is that each person is absolutely lost in the loneliness of their own pain:

It's a grief so great you can't be aware of other people. They're just living. They haven't space for anything but to get through what they're suffering. They'll come out of this, it won't have this intensity, and one hopes the three will support one another; but at the moment, they're half dead, lifeless with sorrow. And yet of course this is the very moment when they're closest to Jesus. The moment when they go as far as they can go into another's death. So it's the most redemptive moment of all.

2 Loneliness in Illness

There are five things which no one is able to accomplish in this world: first, to cease growing old when we are growing old; second, to cease being sick; third, to cease dying; fourth, to deny extinction when there is extinction; fifth, to deny exhaustion. Sooner or later people run into these facts, and most people suffer consequently. But those who have this teaching, do not suffer because they understand these are unavoidable.

(The Teaching of Buddha)

**For medical reasons, I'm confined to a small upstairs flat and
back garden. I can't go to church, go shopping, or to any
indoor social events. I am only 62 and on the scrapheap.'**

(Somerset)

**I became ill with what was later discovered to be ME, and
when I said I was getting worse, they didn't believe me. I felt
very alone, because there was no one I could talk to, who
would listen to what I said and take me seriously. I was scared
that I was going to be taken into care, and nobody was in
contact often enough to know what was going on.**

These two people were struggling with the isolation and loneliness often created by illness. Yet Rosemary Wakelin says now
that her loneliness had one benefit: it stripped away clutter from
her life, and helped her see certain things more clearly:

My daughter had a very terrible illness, and it lasted for several years, which was running concurrently with my husband dying. I was in a very deep abyss really, and I felt I was
at the bottom. There I discovered that if you fight it, the
abyss, if you thrash around, and are struggling all the time,
and feeling this isn't where I should be, all you do is bruise
yourself.

I discovered that the abyss is also worth exploring—or the
darkness, call it what you like. When you're in that state, if
you stop and look around, you become astonished at what
you do find. I found help in incredibly unexpected places—
people that I'd thought might be a help at that sort of time,
when I felt abandoned or in the abyss, actually were no help
at all. Instead, people I had not expected to help me, like my
daughter's teenage friends, for example, did help.

Rosemary had a similar experience earlier on, when a very
unpleasant illness left her with agoraphobia, unable to go out.
Help came not from medical people or adults, but from her four-year-old:

He said, 'Come on Mummy, let's count gates', and managed

to get me to the top of the road, when I couldn't even go out of the front door.'

Over the years, Rosemary's own sense of abandonment at times led her to feel that if Jesus had not given the cry of abandonment on the cross, she could not have remained a Christian:

When things have just been so awful, I've felt that it's only because Jesus felt abandoned himself and said 'My God, my God, why have you forsaken me?' that I can carry on with him, because I know that he knew it too. There is a quote, which goes: 'Down at the bottom of the forgotten world, where God's face never comes, but only man suffers and weeps in the darkness'. That I believe to be profoundly wrong, because it *is* down at the bottom of the forgotten world that God does actually contact us at a very, very deep level.

At midday a darkness fell over the whole land, which lasted till three in the afternoon; and at three Jesus cried aloud, 'Eli, Eli, lema sabachthani?' which means, 'My God, my God, why hast thou forsaken me?' ... Then Jesus gave a loud cry and died. And the curtain of the temple was torn in two from top to bottom. And when the centurion who was standing opposite him saw how he died, he said, 'Truly this man was a son of God.'

Mark 15.33–39 (NEB)

It was the prayers and thoughtfulness of friends that one 58-year-old Cambridgeshire listener says helped her through a fifteen-month period when she was redundant, and felt at times lonely, old, and no longer of use:

There were some days when I would wake up and think 'What am I going to do today?' I lived in an isolated place, and couldn't afford to run my car, so this meant I was unable to do voluntary work. Then so often my telephone would ring and it would be someone saying 'I'm going shopping. Would you like a lift?' or 'There's a meeting in another village. Would you like to come?' No one, unless they are in this position, will understand the pure delight it was for me to be given these gifts.

Others had less happy stories to tell, like a letter-writer from Lincolnshire, now disabled:

What really upset me was the fact that I could not go to the church where I had worshipped for twenty years, because there was no ramp. After six months, a member of the parochial church council ordered one on her own initiative after months of wrangling. There was a lot of bad feeling until it was found that other wheelchair users could see the flower festival and pram pushers were delighted. Now I am allowed to take my wheelchair to the far side of the church and sit away from the congregation by a pillar where I cannot see the choir or altar but am out of the way. I have struggled on feeling desperately isolated, to the extent that I would rather now stay at home and listen to the service on the radio. No wonder if others don't want to join an organisation that is so concerned about the preservation of its buildings that it forgets the needs of the people.

The problem is now resolved. A pew was finally removed, allowing her to sit with the congregation.

But Sister Wendy *chose* what many find so hard—to live completely alone. Those who saw the television series glimpsed her caravan in the woods of an East Anglian convent, from which she emerged to set off with her umbrella. She has no visitors.

I see the nuns over the way from me at morning prayer and at mass. But I don't ever mix with the sisters. Each day, I have about seven hours of prayer and two hours of work, and I read and I think, fortunate me.

Some will find this incredibly strange. 'Aren't people made to be living together in community in one form or another?', I asked.

Yes, it is terribly strange, and people *are* made to be living in community, God made us to be a social creature. It's just that I happen to be one of the very few people who are inadequate. I'm not big enough as a person to cope with the stresses and strains of normal life. So as a kind of therapy, God, who always tempers the wind to the shorn lamb, and sees that he has a real dud here, has taken me to the one place where I can flourish, which is by myself.

Astonishingly, Sister Wendy is never lonely.

I don't know what it means. I have to make a real imaginative leap into this condition that I know causes such untold pain in other people's lives. And I pray about it. I ask God to show the lonely the way out, because he doesn't want people to be lonely.

A long religious tradition exists of people going into the desert to find themselves and to find God—the desert is a place of isolation, stripping away illusions and delusions, recalling the temptations of Jesus in the wilderness. I asked Sister Wendy, Does this spiritual tradition of the desert have anything to say to us now?

Well, I think psychically, emotionally that state might well express what many people feel in their prayer. Many people and some of the holiest people I know, in fact, the holiest person I know, the only saint I've ever met, gets nothing back from God in prayer. She pours herself out, and there's never the faintest flicker of consolation coming from God. And she goes on believing that it's not rock. If you ask your father for bread, will he give you a stone? And you take what looks like a stone, and feels like a stone, and you break your teeth on it, and you say this is bread, because my father gave it to me.

I commented, 'Many people listening may say that's just complete delusion ...'

No, because this is what faith is all about. Faith is believing that God will always help you, whether you feel it or not. That's faith.

Rosemary Wakelin, like me, found that a fairly barren and hard picture:

I'm not sure that I could have had the faith or the discipline to have carried on without being aware of God in a warmer way than that. I think maybe that is the discipline of a very ascetic sort of person ... I know I'm not. My own experience is that often unexpectedly, unasked, I have had experiences, contacts, call them 'God-hugs', moments in your life when you are suddenly aware of something else, which holds you, loves you and makes you feel wonderful.

That was the experience too of a former busy mum and a prison visitor from East Sussex who had fallen ill in the autumn of 1987 and was now bedbound:

> It was and still is very hard to let go. The thing I miss most is going out and giving the world a hug. I feel that I have been in a time-warp—a still place. The rushing world goes on but I am still, as though permanently in the eye of the storm with Jesus and his peace. It made me realise I had lots of acquaintances, but few real friends. Only the dearest come now after so long. I have a loving dear husband, two dear daughters and grandchildren.

Over these years, she had learned that God loves her for herself, not for what she can do or cannot do:

> I have learned too to ask God about what he would like me to do each day. Not always easy. I feel I have become a better listener to people who come to see me ... I think too I have become more gracious.

She used to have great difficulty being on the receiving end of giving—until one day, a very dear friend wanted to bath her on a very hot day:

> I felt I just could not take up her time, until she reminded me about the joy I had felt in the past helping others, and asked would I really want to take that joy away from her now? I know now that I am in a privileged place of prayer which is never interrupted by a busy active life style. I can pray for people night and day. I never realised what a lovely thing that would be.

It sounded as if that listener had found her calling, but Sister Wendy was anxious that we ran the risk of seeming to suggest that a state of uninterrupted prayer, undistracted by the cares that God puts upon us, is a blessed thing for everybody: 'And it isn't. We must live the life we're actually given, and use that specific life to come closer to God.'

For someone isolated and bed-bound through illness, but not drawn to a life of prayer, she suggested things

> that both deepen your own mind and reach out to other people—perhaps writing letters to people in prison, or in hospital, people who would love to hear from somebody. Maybe reading, trying to make a study of something, perhaps taking up an intellectual hobby, like art if you like.

A Somerset listener, who, at 62, regarded herself on the scrap heap through illness, was trying to combine prayer and other activities. She was already writing to a prisoner:

> **I write letters for Amnesty International. I structure my days. I read and pray. Although alone, I don't feel lonely; God is very good in that way. I feel upheld by prayers of people, who understand how it is with me. Recently I have begun to write psalms. I enclose Psalm 3:**

> > *I look for you, O Lord;*
> > *Because the eyes of my mind are dim, I do not see you.*
> > *I see, yet I do not see, because my heart is not given to holiness.*
> > *Let me keep still a little while*
> > *Then I may feel your spirit near me.*
> >
> > *Then, oh then, I may see you*
> > *in all the small things of my life;*
> > *Then my heart may know*
> > *that your love is the cause of all things.*
> > *You are so near to me;*
> > *you are the very breath of my being.*
> >
> > *For you, Lord, have such patience*
> > *with the small things of the earth.*

In the silence,
your heart whispers to my heart;
Your whispers surround my soul like clouds of gold.
You are all about me,
Your tenderness enfolds me like the petals of a rose.
You are for ever in a moment,
and time runs into the arms of eternity.

O Lord, let me walk with you all the days of my life.

3 Long-Term Loneliness

To a disciple who was always seeking answers from him,
the Master said: 'You have within yourself the answer to
every question you propose—if you only knew how to look
for it.' On another occasion, he said: 'In the land of the
spirit, you cannot walk by the light of someone else's
lamp. You want to borrow mine. I would rather teach you
how to make your own.'

———

I'm an elderly spinster, who's been rejected by my entire
family about twenty years ago, for reasons unknown. That's
the rub. I can come to terms with anything if I know what it is I
have to come to terms with. It looks as if I shall go to my
grave without knowing. On official forms which ask for my
next of kin, I've put the name of a firm of solicitors.

(Birmingham)

I've suffered from bereavement, and loss of job, I'm also gay. I
go to church, but I find I want to be apart from people rather
than with people, because I don't feel I belong to any family or
group or organisation, and I think that my anger and
frustration and loneliness all stem from that.

(Hemel Hempstead)

———

At the root of a number of letters from people lonely for years were not only a sense of not belonging, but a lack of self-esteem. As Rosemary Wakelin said, low self-esteem is not the best way of making friends:

> If you think nothing of yourself, you're not going to think very much of other people. An essential part of faith in the Christian religion—and indeed in other faiths—is a proper regard of yourself as God's creature. When you put a value on yourself, you put a value on other people.

The author Monica Furlong once wrote that unless we love ourselves, it is all too natural, when something is offered that may ease our loneliness, to grab, reacting immediately, and so frighten others off. We need somehow to pause, be still, be patient, love ourselves, lay on one side our self-hatred. Then we can begin to respond from a place of inner truth, asking, not grabbing, no longer crushed by a refusal. And maybe sometimes we need to recognise that others are not always to blame. 'There are people' said Rosemary Wakelin, speaking out of years of experience as a Methodist minister, 'who've been so wrapped up in themselves that they've alienated family and potential friends; and haven't seen themselves as friends to other people.'

Yet she does believe that absolutely everyone is needed in some situation or another—and that there are opportunities, wherever we are, to create something better because of what we do and say: 'In the end, my own feeling about life is that you have to be extremely brave. I think life is actually very tough, and we need to have a courage.'

Meditation

In a few moments of quiet, let us bring to mind now:

all whose loneliness is now past, and those whose lives it still envelops ...

We recall our own times of loneliness and of isolation ...

and anything we have read that specially speaks to our own needs.

_____

Lord, so much of our suffering comes from our inability to sit still and be alone. Give us a candle of the Spirit, as we go down into the depths of our being. Use our times of solitude to rid us of our illusions, to take us to the spring of our life, and to hear the voice of our own hearts. We ask this in the name of Jesus, who also experienced the desert.

* * * * * * * * *

(Music)

* * * * * * * * *

Lord, you walk before us wherever we go—even into the utmost depths of desolation. On the day of crucifixion, the subject of taunts and jeers, even you felt utterly alone. Walk before us now into the path of light and peace.

_____

For the darkness of waiting
of not knowing what is to come
of staying steady and quiet and attentive,
we praise you, O God:

All: For the darkness and the light
are both alike to you.

For the darkness of choosing
when you give us the moment
to speak, and act, and change,
and we cannot know what we have set in motion,
but we still have to take the risk,
we praise you, O God:

All: For the darkness and the light
are both alike to you.

> (from *Litany of Waiting*, Janet Morley)

* * * * * * * *

(Song)

* * * * * * * *

Lord, it is easy enough to ask you to give us the energy to change
the world, or even our family and friends. But Lord, we ask for
something much more difficult—the grace to change ourselves.
Help us to begin at the beginning, so that in the days and years
ahead, we do not waste what is left of our lives.

Lord, we ask forgiveness

for abandoning others, for being self-absorbed.
for all we have done to isolate others
for all we have not done

Help us to look for ways that can break our isolation,
help us to ask not grab,
to be no longer crushed by refusals
to use our solitude to get to know ourselves and you better.

———

God of love and forgiveness
Save us by your tenderness
From each deed of evilness,
From each act of sinfulness
From each thought of carelessness

From each idea of wickedness
From each word of hurtfulness
From each speech of harmfulness

Save us by your tenderness
God of love and forgiveness.

(St Hilda Community)

* * * * * * * *

(Song)

* * * * * * * *

Lord, we pray for all those afflicted by loneliness, even in the midst of companionship.

We pray for all those cut off from family and friends and home, specially for those isolated by terror—in Bosnia, in Africa, ... in so many other places.

We pray for all people of God
in this country and around the world.
May they be part of the answer to our problems,
not part of the problem itself.

May we create places of honesty,
where loneliness is not denied,
and places of courage
where people feel free to share their real experience.

———

Lord's Prayer or alternative version:

God, who cares for us,
The wonder of whose presence fills us with awe.
Let kindness, justice and love shine in our world.
Let your secrets be known here as they are in heaven.
Give us the food and the hope we need for today.
Forgive us our wrongdoing

as we forgive the wrongs done to us.
Protect us from pride and despair
and from the fear and hate which can swallow us up.
In you is truth, meaning, glory and power,
while worlds come and go. Amen.

(Monica Furlong)

Creator God, you know what we need, without our words.
Hear our prayer and hear also our silence.
Grant us those things we cannot or dare not voice.
We make these prayers through our brother Jesus. Amen.

Finally, God's promise that there is a way through the wilderness:

I will make a way even through the wilderness
and paths in the barren desert;
the wild beasts shall do me honour,
the wolf and the ostrich;
for I will provide water in the wilderness
and rivers in the barren desert.

Isaiah 43. 19–20 (NEB)

May the Lord bless us and keep us
May the Lord make his face to shine upon us
And be gracious unto us.
May the Lord lift up the light of his countenance upon us
And give us his peace. Amen.

* * * * * * *

Some Suggestions for Worship Music

1 Song: 'I Will Wait' by Maggi Dawn, from LP *Follow* (Kingsway Music).

2 'The Orient' by Dick Walter, from CD *The Editor's Companion 5* (KPM).

3 'Cosmos' by Shaw/Rogers, from *Space* (Carlin).

4 Song: 'God Beyond All Names' by Bernadette Farrell (OCP).

5 'The Lord Bless You and Keep You' from *Gloria: the Sacred Music of John Rutter* (OUP and Collegium Records).

Other Music

6 'In the Winter' by Janis Ian, from LP *Between the Lines* (CBS).

7 'Heartstrings' by Dick Walter, from *The Editor's Companion* (KPM).

8 'Crucifixus' by J. S. Bach, from *Mass in B Minor.*

9 'Flos Campi—Suite' by Vaughan Williams, from CD *Symphony no. 5 in D.*

****

DR SHEILA CASSIDY works at Plymouth General Hospital as Palliative Care Specialist. Between 1982 and 1993 she was Director of St Luke's Hospice in Plymouth. She qualified in medicine in 1963 at Oxford University, and then embarked initially on a career in plastic surgery. In 1975, she was detained and tortured in Chile for treating a wounded revolutionary, and spent two months in prison, before being expelled. After her return, she was very active in human rights work, lecturing widely at home and abroad. In 1978, she entered a convent, but left after eighteen months, returning to full-time medical work.

Her main interest in medicine now is the emotional and spiritual care of cancer patients. She is particularly interested in the relationship between doctors and patients. She has written five books, reflecting on her experiences. A sixth is an illustrated creation myth.

KATHY GALLOWAY is a theologian and writer who works with a wide variety of groups—both secular and religious. Keenly interested in new forms of community, she lived for six years in a basic Christian community in Edinburgh. Kathy Galloway is a member of the Iona Community, a former warden of Iona Abbey, and currently edits the community's magazine Coracle.

Over the years, she has campaigned for a Scottish Parliament, for an Edinburgh Peace and Justice Resource Centre, and for various justice and anti-poverty causes. She is now chairperson of CommonWeal, a Scottish organisation seeking to promote justice.

She has published poetry, worship material and writing on spirituality and liberation. Her collection of poems and lyrics, Love Burning Deep, and her most recent book, Struggles to Love: the Spirituality of the Beatitudes, are published by SPCK. She lives with her three children in Glasgow.

TWO
Fear

One day a disciple asked the Master: 'What is the greatest enemy of enlightenment?' The Master sat silently. Then, he said, 'Fear'. 'And where does fear come from?' asked the disciple. 'Delusion', replied the Master. The disciple looked puzzled: 'And what is delusion?' he asked. 'To think that flowers around you are poisonous snakes,' said the Master. 'Open your eyes and see.'

Two years ago, I had the all-clear after surgery for breast cancer, and now I've found another lump, and I'm so afraid.

I moved a year ago to live in a village. No-one wants to accept me into the community and I dread having to live with all the gossip about me.

(Scotland)

I am one of the long-term unemployed. I lie awake at night worrying about what's going to become of me and my family. I can't see any way out.

(Scotland)

It can be fear of being in someone else's power; fear of what other people think; fear of failing, and being seen to fail, at work or at home; fear of illness, and dying—whatever the circumstances, the effect can be devastating.

And all these different fears can be found in the Passion story:

the fears of those who hated Jesus, the fears of the disciples, the fears of Jesus himself in the Garden of Gethsemane.

So is fear inevitable? Is it a part of being human? or a useful warning against unsafe actions? If so, how do we distinguish between the sort that recognises poisonous snakes for what they are, and the useless fear that deludes us into seeing snakes where they are only flowers? And how do we find the courage to face fear and overcome it?

1 Fear of Violence

In the letters we received, most disturbing of all was the fear and experience of utter powerlessness:

> There have been two occasions in my life when I feared I would lose my liberty for crimes I did not commit. I could not escape, there was nothing I could do to save myself. How would I cope? What would become of my family?
>
> (Fife)

> My husband tried to kill me three times over a period of ten years. He even tried to push me in front of a train twice ... but others saw it. At first I thought it was my fault. But in the eighth year of our marriage, my husband attacked a female manager in his office and was taken to hospital in some sort of derangement ... The consultant told me my husband had a rare mental disorder.
>
> (Bromley)

> I had been sexually abused as a child, and the abuser had been my own mother. It was very scary. I really thought I was going mad, because I didn't know of anybody else who had the same experience.

———

These all described extreme situations, but to Kathy Galloway, the *fear* of physical threat is widespread, particularly among women. She knows someone who was raped by a number of men:

For years, the fear of that meant she would not leave her house, she was just so frightened. Eventually through contact and support, she started to go out, but she only goes out if there's somebody with her. The disablement of that attack is far more than the attack itself—the physical wounds heal, but the scars you carry; and so many people live in situations of external real tangible threat—their fears are justified, their environment is very hostile.

Bullying is feared—among both children and adults. One letter came from a former child evacuee during the Second World War, who wrote to say that apart from the fear of darkness due to the blackout and gas lights, he was often bullied by older boys after lights out in the dormitory, as he was one of the youngest.

Another story illustrated a form of bullying too:

> I found out that the firm I work for is paying much more than it needs to for parts for the product we make, and when I told the head of my department, he told me it wasn't doing me any harm, and if I made a fuss about it, I'd find myself out of a job. I'm frightened to go any higher up on this, because I'm pretty sure our management is going along with it. And I'd lose my job, and I'm scared to resign because I'm 54, and where would I get another job at my age? I'm not sure how to live with myself if I don't stand up against what I believe to be wrong, but I'm frightened of what'll happen to my family if I do.

Several letters described fear at work—not just the fear of being out of a job, but of becoming a party, however unwillingly, to shady or unjust behaviour, and not being sure what to do. Kathy Galloway commented that when jobs get fewer, the pressure to conform gets stronger and stronger:

> You go to interviews, and you think, 'Now what should I say? What do people want me to say in order to get this job?' So you lose part of yourself in that. Or maybe you don't speak up—not even necessarily about corrupt practices, but just you're afraid to take any kind of risks in your work. All the time, you're playing it safe.

Today, more and more big institutions—like schools, the health service, the media, and industry—seem to include and enforce clauses in employees' contracts forbidding them to speak publicly, without special permission, about what is going on in their place of work. Sheila Cassidy thought that could soon be happening to her: 'The hospital where I work has just become an NHS trust, and I think that's the case in some trusts, so I don't know how I'll react to it.' She added, with a rueful half-laugh, that she imagined she would sign.

One paradox is that people who appear to others to be in positions of power may see themselves as powerless and afraid:

When Krushchev pronounced his famous denunciation of Stalin, someone in the Congress Hall is reported to have said, 'Where were you, Comrade Kruschev, when all those innocent people were being slaughtered?'

Krushchev paused, looking round the Hall, and said, 'Will the person who said that kindly stand up!'

Tension mounted in the hall. No one moved.

Said Krushchev: 'Well, whoever you are, you have your answer now. I was in exactly the same position then as you find yourself now.'
                    (from Song of the Bird, *Anthony de Mello)*

The most profound depth of fear Kathy Galloway had experienced was not to do with a real tangible threat, but with a nameless fear, when you do not know what is going to happen. 'Not knowing and your imagining are far worse.'

St Peter discovered that, when, faced with hostile questioning after Jesus's arrest, he realised that what he had boasted of doing, and what he in fact would do, were worlds apart:

[And Peter said], 'Lord, I am ready to go with you to prison and death.' Jesus said, 'I tell you, Peter, the cock will not crow tonight until you have three times over denied that you know me.' ...

Then they arrested him and led him away. They brought

*him to the High Priest's house, and Peter followed at a
distance. They lit a fire in the middle of the courtyard and
sat round it, and Peter sat among them. A serving-maid
who saw him sitting in the firelight stared at him and said,
'This man was with him too.' But he denied it: 'Woman,'
he said, 'I do not know him.' A little later someone else
noticed him and said, 'You also are one of them.' But Peter
said to him, 'No, I am not.' About an hour passed and
another spoke more strongly still: 'Of course this fellow
was with him. He must have been; he is a Galilean.' But
Peter said, 'Man, I do not know what you are talking
about.' At that moment, while he was still speaking, a cock
crew; and the Lord turned and looked at Peter. And Peter
remembered the Lord's words, 'Tonight before the cock
crows, you will disown me three times.'*

Luke 22.33–4; 54–61 (NEB)

In the courtyard by the fire, maybe Peter rationalised to himself
that he would be much better keeping his head down, and be of
more help to Jesus too. After all, if he could find out what was
happening, and remain free, he might be of use. What was the
use of unnecessarily risking torture and death?

To Sheila Cassidy, the story has a special personal signifi-
cance:

> Once, when I was on a retreat, I was drawing the story. I had
> Peter saying he didn't know Jesus, and then sitting with his
> shoulders bowed, weeping outside the court. Then I found
> myself drawing another apocryphal picture with Jesus in
> chains on his way to Calvary with his arm round Peter's
> shoulder, comforting him; and it was almost as though Jesus
> was saying to him: 'It's all right, Peter, I understand that you
> couldn't hold on.' That was very special for me, because
> when I was being tortured, I couldn't hold on, and my
> betrayal led to the arrest of a number of priests. I felt very
> guilty about that for a long time, until I realised that in fact
> I had held on as long as anyone—or as long as I—humanly
> could, and all one can do is all one can do.

Finally, even Peter's betrayal was turned to good effect. His
shame at his fear was the spur to make amends, to be worthy of

his boast. For the rest of his life, he spread the good news of the resurrection of Christ.

When Sheila Cassidy treated the wounded man in Chile, she did so, aware of possible serious consequences, though torture did not occur to her:

> I was more frightened that I would be found out and thrown out of the country. I think I thought there was a fleeting chance that I might be killed, because we'd been warned that the house where I treated the wounded revolutionary could be suddenly invaded by the secret police.

So, looking back, did she now think she had been naïve? Was her fear a healthy, warning fear?

> I think it was a healthy naïveté, because I think it made it easier for me to do it. I still think, I still hope, that I would have done it even had I known what was going to happen to me, because I'm utterly convinced it was the right thing to do.

The Indian poet, Tagore, prayed, 'Let me not pray to be sheltered from dangers, but to be fearless in facing them'; but to Sheila, real courage is acting constructively even if you are afraid: 'And I'm quite sure the United Nations soldiers and all those aid workers in Bosnia and other similar places are absolutely terrified; but they manage to override their terror because of their need to help.'

Even famous people who give the public impression of total confidence, have periods of private fear. Martin Luther King, for instance, the black American civil rights leader, knew perfectly well the risk of his eventual assassination:

> *I sat there and thought about a beautiful little daughter who had just been born ... I started thinking about a dedicated, devoted and loyal wife, who was over there asleep ... And I discovered that religion had to become real to me, and I had to know God for myself. I bowed down over that cup of coffee, I never will forget it ... I prayed a prayer and I prayed out loud that night ... 'I'm losing my courage. And I can't let the people see me like this because if they see me weak and losing my courage,*

*they will begin to get weak' ... And it seemed at that
moment that I could hear an inner voice saying to me,
'Martin Luther, stand up for righteousness. Stand up for
justice. Stand up for truth. And lo, I will be with you, even
until the end of the world.' He promised never to leave me,
never to leave me alone. No, never alone.*

Rabbi Lionel Blue, in his book *Day Trip to Eternity*, put it this
way: 'The presence of God is not our air-raid shelter, but our
launching-pad into the unknown and the dark. In our religious
organisations, we are God's commercial travellers. We do not sell
insurance, but courage, the courage to face reality and deal with
it honestly.'

After all, say the rabbis, when Moses threw the wand into the
Red Sea, the sea, quite contrary to the expected miracle, did not
divide itself to leave a dry passage for the Jews. Not until the first
man had jumped into the sea did the promised miracle happen
and waves recede.

2 Fear of What Other People Think

When I was a child, I hardly ever seemed to think much about
the impression I made on other people. But after about the age of
thirteen, and for long after that, I worried about what people
thought. It took me years to realise that if I was true to my best
vision of myself, then it mattered less and less what others
thought.

My anxieties always seemed to emerge more when meeting
unknown people, unknown situations. As a member of
Scotland's Iona Community and a group called CommonWeal,
Kathy Galloway tries as part of her work, to break down anxieties that occur when people who hardly ever meet begin to
communicate with each other—politicians with those who are
too disillusioned even to vote; artists with people who have
never tried painting or entered an art gallery; church leaders
with those alienated from the Church.

I think fear plays a big part for anybody faced with a group,
or a situation, or individuals who are so different they present some kind of a threat, so that, if you're going to meet
them, you have to step outside where you feel comfortable
and safe. If you're going to meet people who are very differ-

ent, then you really have to draw away from your place of safety, your secure rock, and that's very frightening.

The single most important thing that helped her deal with fear was a dream she had when she was about 21 or 22:

> I think it must have been quite a fearful time for me. I dreamt I was in my house and there was a tapping at the window. I opened the curtain and there was this shapeless creature outside the window, tapping and tapping and tapping, and howling to get in. In every room I ran to in the house this creature appeared, as if it were going round the house from the outside. I was absolutely terrified, and all of a sudden, I just had this certainty that what I had to do was to open the window and let it in; and it jumped into my arms, and instead of being this horrible, shapeless, frightening thing, it became really pathetic, and sad, and kind of lovable; and I felt then that the dream was saying that the thing to do with my fears was to try and embrace them. That's what I've lived out of ever since. I don't always succeed, but for me that dream was a gift from God.

The lives of some people have for centuries been affected and shaped by the ignorance, fear and hostility of others. Many gay and lesbian people, for instance, have felt forced to hide part of themselves and their lives from others, out of fear of aggression, so becoming vulnerable to another fear—the fear of being discovered. Matthew Parris, the former Tory MP, has now freed himself from that fear by no longer hiding his sexual orientation. When he was still an MP, he was terrified of the press discovering his secret:

> I'm not suggesting I was leading a desperately exciting or dangerous or even sinful life, but I knew there were things about me which if other people knew could get into the press and destroy me. So you're never completely relaxed, there's always something nagging in the back of your mind. I went into a gay pub in South London, and I was standing there, having a drink, and this fellow came up to me. I thought I'd seen him somewhere before, and he said, 'Are you Matthew Parris, MP?' and my blood chilled, and my heart stopped. I said 'Yes'. There didn't seem a lot of point denying it. He told

me he was a lobby correspondent, at the House of Commons, and I thought, 'Oh no, this is the end. I've been found; they've been putting people out in the pubs and clubs to catch me, and they've caught me.' Of course, it wasn't so at all. He was gay too, and he was in the pub for a drink just like me. He was just being friendly.

I suppose when people use the word fear, one thinks of the immediate intense physical fear of sudden danger, that sort of heart-pumping and adrenalin. That of course is a desperately shocking and intense sort of feeling, but for my money I would much rather experience small moments of intense physical fear in my life, than those long periods of low-level, nagging-in-the-back-of-your-mind kind of fear that I experienced as an MP.

3 Fear of Failing

Everybody at work tells me I'm good at my job, but I find it a lot more difficult to do than any of them seem to, and despite what they say, I just know one day I'll do something terrible and be found out. The trouble is that the more they try to encourage me and tell me how well I'm doing, the more I feel what a struggle it is to do the job at all, never mind well.

(Edinburgh)

Had Sheila Cassidy ever felt that?

Oh, so much. I think the tragedy is that so many people pretend to be completely whole, completely knowledgeable, completely pure, whereas so many of us, for example, have been depressed. I was terrified that people would find out I was having psychotherapy, that I'd been depressed and that I couldn't sleep, because I felt that, in a sense, I wasn't doing my job properly. I found the courage in recent months and years to be able to say, 'Okay, I have been badly depressed, actually I'm still on anti-depressants, but I'm really well now', and I think it's very important to be able to speak openly about these things, about child abuse, about depression, about schizophrenia, about cancer, so that people can know there is life after mental illness, physical illness, abuse.

What helped get her to the point where she could talk openly about it was writing a book:

> The first half was very well defended; it was all scriptural, all about the care of the dying. Then right in the middle, I got very badly depressed, and I couldn't write at all. After six weeks I started to write again; but the only stuff that would come was from very deep down. So the book took off in a completely new direction—very much more open, vulnerable, in a stripping sort of way. I still get letters almost every day about that book. I realised how immensely affirming it was to other people, and then I realised how I was infinitely safer, because there was nothing more for people to find out about me. If I declare that I spend too much on clothes, I eat too much chocolate, I don't pray enough, I pick my nose, and I'm depressed and take anti-depressants, well really, I'm as bad as the next woman!

My own early fears of failing were linked to failing exams, or of becoming trapped in uncongenial work; but there are worse things than failing exams—like failing in generosity or imagination, or sensitivity.

I found it helpful when someone pointed out that we use jobs; jobs do not use us. Unsatisfactory jobs are stepping stones to something else, convenient suppliers of income until something better emerges. Jobs themselves cannot define or diminish us, unless we allow them to do so.

Moreover, even if we do not get the job we want, then Nancy Seabrooke, aged 79, who was an understudy for years in Agatha Christie's West End play *The Mousetrap*, has a point. She said that if you are not chosen for a part, it is because they liked the other person, and not because you yourself failed in some traumatic way.

To many, worst of all is the fear of failing the family. A Luton listener was told her baby daughter (now aged twelve) had a rare liver disease that could be life-threatening. To begin with, she and her husband were able to accept the news with the help of prayer:

> **As we prayed, we were enabled in a moment of grace to give her back to God, having realised that we are only the**

guardians of our children, they belong to God. It seems He
gave us her back and at that moment when we prayed we
were given that 'peace which passes understanding'—we were
flooded with it, as it were, from head to foot.

But four months later, when the baby was going to be allowed
home from the hospital, she became gripped with fear:

How would I cope with this condition without doctors and
nurses nearby? A book helped me realise that Jesus
continually says 'Do not fear'. So for three days, I prayed,
'Lord, I don't feel as if I'm not afraid, but I'm just going to
believe it's possible.' On the third day, she was discharged
and I was no longer afraid.

Kathy Galloway's sharpest sense of failing came when her marriage broke up:

It's such a terrible thing, particularly in church circles. So
you're dealing with paroxysms of fear, of having your entire
life-map torn up, and also the fear for your children. That's
a factor in a lot of the fear we've talked about—sometimes
you don't do things because you fear for other people, not
just for yourself. You're afraid of how your actions will
affect them. But the kind of expectations that people in the
church feel—that you have to be strong, you have to be
cheerful and you have to be positive all the time—these can
be terribly weighty.

Very small things helped her through that:

I found it very helpful just to pour myself into the present
moment, and to pay a lot of attention to small sensory
things. There was a tree outside my window, which I used
to watch. I spent a long time sitting looking at the leaves on
the tree. It was calming, and it also brought me into the present. Because the past had been changed, it was all full of
fear; and the future too was full of fear. So the only thing
was the present, and very concrete things like smells and
senses and conversations, and just trying not to take on
everything at once, but just to live not even a day at a time,
but a moment at a time, a few minutes at a time.

A Japanese warrior was captured and thrown into prison.
At night he could not sleep for he was convinced he would
be tortured next morning. Then the words of his Master
came to him: 'Tomorrow is not real. The only reality is
now.' So he came to the present and fell asleep.
                     (from Song of the Bird, *Anthony de Mello*)

4 Fear of Pain or Illness or Dying

At the moment I am suffering from leukaemia and so I am
very, very afraid. I shouldn't be because I'm a former nurse, a
state registered nurse. I do experience dreadfully the sense of
isolation along with my fear. I have a loving and devoted
husband, but we are both very frightened and sometimes too
scared to speak about it to each other. I have my children and
they have shown caring, but we don't want to be a burden on
them. I love them dearly, but I think we are, or at least I am,
experiencing the feeling of being lost.

This was one of many calls and letters about the fear of pain,
death, and the unknown. Today, Dr Sheila Cassidy is a specialist in hospice care and relieving those in pain. She reckons that
almost everyone she works with feels at some point terribly
afraid:

When people facing death first realise it's coming, they're
utterly terrified, and what they need is someone to be beside
them—to be, in a sense, a rock, a secure base. And then, as
they get nearer and are able to confront it, then sometimes
or very often that fear goes.

Some people suffer pathological anxiety—anxiety as a disease,
when people feel giddy, cannot see straight, feel physically sick,
as Dr Sheila Cassidy has experienced:

When I was beginning to consider going back to Chile, I was
on a train, and was suddenly overcome by this terrible,
nameless dread. I thought I was going to die. It was a hor-
rendous fear of annihilation, and that was my first experience of it. My unconscious mind was thinking about how
narrowly I'd escaped death before, and how going back to
Chile would put me at risk. I think that kind of fear is the
nauseating terror felt by people who are really facing death.

But it was not just death, but the whole process of medical treatment, that some listeners wrote in to describe:

I had to have a brain scan. I was terrified of being left alone, and I have a phobia about being fastened down in any way on my back. I thought I'd be reassured by the nurses and doctors on duty through the little window from their room to the scan room, but they were all laughing and joking and ignoring me completely. I lay there, shaking with fear and I honestly thought I might die of fright. I felt that God had absolutely and utterly withdrawn, and despite my trust in Him had abandoned me, leaving me to experience the full force of terror.

That Solihull listener found a way through the nightmare:

My husband and I prayed our way through each of our hospital experiences later. We pictured in prayer each situation where I'd been afraid, and then we tried to imagine by faith Jesus himself or an angel standing there beside me all the time. I found it very helpful.

To Kathy Galloway, these ways of imagining or visualising situations are really important: 'I think it's good to recognise them even though they don't sound very sensible or rational. They're like gifts, like the things that come out when we paint, or in music or poetry, because they release the fear, so that we can look at it.'

Other listeners, even without such visualising, found their fear replaced quite suddenly, and unexpectedly, by a sense of peace:

Last year I faced fear when I'd been off work for nine months going through quite a severe depression. I was back at work for a day or two and then waking up in the middle of the night one night vomiting blood and being frightened. But even as the ambulance was being called, I suddenly felt a great peace. And the next day, when I thought the waiting would be a time of apprehension and worry, God gave me such a wonderful quality of peace. I had no fear, no apprehension, the fear just wasn't there that I would otherwise have felt. Just to know I can latch into that peace has helped me through what was such a traumatic experience.

Common to all such letters was an experience of letting go of fear, recognising that it helped not at all.

One day, I asked the Master, 'How shall I rid myself of fear?'
He answered: 'Rid yourself of what you cling to.'
'You mean I actually cling to my fears?'
'Consider what you fear protects you from,' he said, 'and you will agree. And you will see your folly.'

Some listeners even found that letting go of their fears released a happiness they had never known before. A university teacher from Leeds was in 1989 diagnosed as having cancer in the pancreas, and was told, incorrectly as it turned out, that she would die soon:

When I was first told I was about to die, I thought, 'Right. This is it. What do I pray for? Life? But why should God intervene in the laws of nature just to save me? Lots of far better, more important people than I will die—like the mothers and fathers of small children. Anyway dying's not the worst thing that can happen.' I went on in this way for a while, still acting the competent, in-command person I had always been until I realised how laughable that was.

At that point I decided that it was all too complicated for me. So, as I lay there, I gathered up all the complications like a tangled skein of wool and, very vividly in my mind, lifted them up, and deposited the lot in God's lap, saying: 'Look, I can't handle this. *You* do what you think is best and that'll be fine by me. My only prayer is, do not abandon me to chance. I don't care what happens to me as long as it's what you decide.'

And so I relaxed completely and surrendered myself to God. Fleeting images of a small boat, launching out onto an enormous ocean without sails or oars came to me and I accepted them ... After this, I felt totally at peace and *safe*.

Nothing could harm me ... When I was sent home to die, that summer was the happiest of my life.

The image of the sea spoke to another listener, also recovered from cancer:

From my hospital bed, I see the sea, Mumbles Head, the lifeboat house and the lighthouse. The lighthouse winks its message all night to mariners—warns them, guides them round the rocky point into Swansea harbour ... Lord, how it reminds me of you. Safety, rescue and a final haven of peace.

After my mother's death at the end of a long illness, I found these words of St Francis de Sales on a card in her handbag:

Do not look forward to what may happen tomorrow. The same everlasting father who cares for you today will take care of you tomorrow and every day. Either God will shield you from suffering, or God will give you unfailing strength to bear it. Be at peace then, and put aside all anxious thoughts and imaginings.

Meditation

In a few moments of quiet, let us bring to mind:

all whose fear is now past, and those whose lives it still
envelops.

We recall our own fears ...

and anything we have read that specially speaks to our own
needs.

****

(Music)

****

Loving Lord,
you knew the prison of fear,
the pain of torture.
Just as you came risen and unexpected
to those first friends of yours
who deserted you
and who hid behind closed doors in their deep fear,
be with us now,
and touch us with your peace.

———

Have no fear; for I have paid your ransom;
I have called you by name and you are my own.
When you pass through deep waters, I am with you,
when you pass through rivers,
they will not sweep you away;
walk through fire and you will not be scorched,
through flames and they will not burn you,
For I am the Lord your God,
the Holy One of Israel, your deliverer.
                                    Isaiah 43.1–3 (NEB)

The angel said, 'Do not be afraid.'

Luke 2.10 (NEB)

————

O God our deliverer,
at whose feet we are free
to lay down our heavy burden:

we bring before you ...

(You could pray about your own fears, those who have made you afraid, those mentioned in the news who are fearful, those maybe you yourself have frightened. This is what Kathy, Sheila and I prayed for ...)

Sheila: We pray for those who cannot sleep because they have cancer, because they are afraid of being deserted, or of losing their jobs ... Lord, give them courage.

Rosemary: We pray for those who are afraid of growing old ...

Kathy: We pray for those who are afraid of being different, attracting attention, attracting hostility ... We pray for freedom in our fears.

Sheila: We pray for those who live in a situation of ongoing fear, for people in Northern Ireland, in Bosnia, for people afraid of the spectre of famine.

Kathy: We pray for people who live in a climate of violence where streets and authorities and structures are hostile or dangerous.

Rosemary: We pray too for people at work who see injustice around them, who feel uncertain of how to confront it.

————

Lord, help us not to be overcome by self-pity, or bitterness or resentment.

We ask forgiveness for all those times we judged others, condemning those things we did not understand.

We ask forgiveness for assuming we knew all there was to know about others, for presuming to speak for others, for defining, confining, labelling, interpreting and oppressing others.

Holy God,
whose name is not honoured
where the needy are not served,
and the powerless are treated with contempt:
may we embrace our neighbours
whether near or far
with the same tenderness
that we ourselves require;
so your justice may be fulfilled in your love,
through Jesus Christ, Amen.

(Janet Morley)

* * * * * * * *

(Song)

* * * * * * * *

Loving Lord, of darkness and of light,
we are afraid of being changed.

We ask you to shake us.
but we fear being broken.
we ask you to challenge us,
but we cannot handle our guilt.
we ask you to work in us,
but we fear being disturbed into action.
We ask you to bless us,
but we fear being made whole.

(Neill Thew)

Spirit of comfort and longing,
enfold our fear,
unclothe us of our pride,
unweave our thoughts,
and uncomplicate our hearts.
Help us to be always hopeful
gardeners of the spirit
who know that without darkness
nothing comes to birth
as without light
nothing flowers.

(Iona Community)

Creed

We believe in God ... yes ... we do believe that there is someone
who brought us to this day and leads us to another ... sometimes
in darkness, sometimes in light. A God who loves the world and
all its people of every kind and creed, including us.

We believe in Jesus Christ, son of God, who lived two thousand
years ago in Palestine, and yet, who amazingly lives among us,
here and now.

We believe in the Holy Spirit ... we do believe that there is a
presence that breathes deeply within us ... stirs restless longings
... measures out a new rhythm to our lives, and draws us
towards one another.

We believe in the community of God, if that means we believe in
people; in Peter, in Mary, in Francis from Asissi, and we believe
they dreamed, and suffered, and loved, in faith.

We believe in a pilgrim Church, in a living, breathing, struggling
group of people who walk together, sometimes in peace, sometimes in conflict, in search of the light of God's truth.

We believe in life everlasting. Amen.

* * * * * * * *

(Music)

* * * * * * * *

Finally a reading from Paul's letter to the Christians at Philippi:

Do not be anxious about anything, but in everything, by prayer and petition, with thanksgiving, present your requests to God. And the peace of God, which transcends all understanding, will guard your hearts and your minds in Christ Jesus.

Finally ... whatever is true, whatever is noble, whatever is right, whatever is pure, whatever is lovely, whatever is admirable—if anything is excellent or praiseworthy—think about such things ... And the God of peace will be with you.

Philippians 4. 6–9 (NIV)

****

Some Suggestions for Worship Music

1 'The Resting Place on the Hill' by Aaron Copland.
2 'Venus' by Gustav Holst, from *The Planet Suite, op. 32.*
3 Song: 'A Touching Place', by John Bell and Graham Maule (Wild Goose Publications).
4 *Psalm 91*, music by John Bell (Wild Goose Publications).
5 *Concerto for Clarinet*, second movement, by Finzi.

Other Music

6 'Boadicea' by Enya, from LP *The Celts* (EMI Songs Ltd/WEA).
7 'Lament' by David Darling, from LP *David Darling Cello* (ECM).
8 *Sonata for Two Violins, op. 56* by Prokofiev.
9 'Gentle Dark-Eyed Mary' (traditional, arranged by Cronshaw/Sanders) from *The Andrew Cronshaw CD* (MCPS/Cloud Valley Music).
10 *Sinfonietta, op. 60*, Janacek.

****

LIONEL BLUE *is a lecturer at the Leo Baeck College, a seminary for European rabbis, and a former convenor of the religious court of the Reform Synagogues of Great Britain. Well-known through his popular regular contributions to BBC Radio 4's* Thought for the Day, *he has also written many books including* A Backdoor to Heaven *(an autobiography),* To Heaven with Scribes and Pharisees, *and* Forms of Prayer *(with co-editor Rabbi Dr Jonathan Magonet).*

DR JOHN SENTAMU *was born in 1947 into a large family in Uganda. He qualified first as a barrister, and between 1972 and 1974, was a judge in the High Court of Uganda. In 1973, he was imprisoned for three months under General Amin, accused incorrectly of helping someone to escape, and beaten up by Amin's soldiers. In 1974, he came to Britain to take a degree in theology, and was ordained an Anglican priest after the murder of Archbishop Luwum, his Ugandan Archbishop, in 1977. For three years, he worked as a chaplain in a remand centre for young male offenders. He is now a priest in South London.*

THREE

Anger

One right is guaranteed to everybody:
To call this short unhappy life his own;
To take a bit of pleasure with the shoddy,
And when he asks for bread to eat not get a stone.
This human right belongs to everybody.
But sad to say it never yet has happened
That things should go the way they ought to go.
Who wouldn't want a little decent treatment?
It seems that circumstance won't have it so ...

(The Threepenny Opera, *Bertolt Brecht)*

My husband and elder son aged just three and half, were wiped out in a horrific road accident by a driver who was an uninsured learner. I remember attending the inquest and seeing the perpetrators of this misery sitting stony-faced and unmoved by the court. If only they'd made one gesture of sympathy or contrition towards me, I could have forgiven then, but even now, I find it a bitter choking experience to think about.

(Solihull)

About eight years ago I had an affair. He left his wife, but he wouldn't do anything to make our relationship permanent. Eventually I broke the relationship. But I was so angry. I wanted to burn his house down, and plotted ways to blow up his car.

(Derby)

I'm a professional person with a good salary, apparently successful. But my life has been clouded by a recurrent difficulty in coping with anger.

(West Yorkshire)

There was a period of about eleven months, when my husband was trying to make up his mind whether he should leave to live with another woman. One day she telephoned me to taunt me saying that I had missed my chance, and that she had won. It was an incredible call, leaving me almost gasping with anger, jealousy and frustration. I remember flinging myself down at the foot of the bed. There were no words, just this dreadful loathsome feeling.

(London)

A few people say they never get angry; but everyone else knows the symptoms—that pounding heart, the mushrooming energy, the pleasurable (usually misleading) sense of self-righteousness, and then (maybe) the releasing explosion, which, if expressed badly and inappropriately, can cause more long-term problems than it solves.

One of anger's paradoxes is that it often flares out most at people we love most, of whom we have such high expectations. Repeated daily irritations may trigger anger, or sometimes long-suppressed painful family incidents that took place long ago. But often those closest to us also get the unpleasant backwash of our anger at others with whom we dare not be so frank. After all, those we love should in theory be able to stand the onslaught, and love us enough to take it on board.

A deeper anger is the kind anchored in historic social and religious injustices that go back centuries, involving not just ourselves and our families, but generations, even our whole race.

As a Jew, Lionel Blue knows of that anger. He hardly gives the impression of an angry person, but in fact he has experienced intense anger in his life. He reckons he has felt angry with almost everybody at one time or another, but specially with the people he has loved, clergy of his own faith, the clergy of other faiths, and with God too.

The worst anger came in his childhood with the experience of poverty. His father was a master tailor. He lost his job in the great depression and was unemployed for the next five or six years. So Lionel's mother had to take a job.

It destroyed my father's dignity, and it nearly broke up their marriage. What really got me was that my mother wanted to get me out of the ghetto, so we had to visit our rich relations. And the iron really burnt into me then. It wasn't poverty, it was the feeling that you were singled out, that it was unfair, and I suppose that was a cause of a large part of my later involvement in politics.

When John Sentamu came to Britain, he encountered a very different attitude to anger compared with what he knew in Uganda. At home, he and his brothers and sisters had been allowed to express their emotions, whatever they were, and they did not bottle them up. 'Whereas here, when we arrived, if something made me very angry, and I told somebody "You've really annoyed me", they thought you were slightly uncivilised. You do not voice what you are actually feeling inside. So I found it wasn't very healthy.'

Letters we received described anger at many different things: violence, racism, poverty, unemployment, being rejected at home or at work, and anger at God.

1 Anger at Violence

Buddha was once threatened with death by a bandit called Angulimala.

'Then be good enough to fulfil my dying wish,' said Buddha.

'Cut off the branch of that tree.' One slash of the sword, and it was done! 'What now?' asked the bandit.

'Put it back again,' said the Buddha. The bandit laughed. 'You must be crazy to think that anyone can do that.'

'On the contrary, it is you who are crazy to think that you are mighty because you can wound and destroy. That

is the task of children. The mighty know how to create and heal.'

I've recently had an experience which has turned our life upside down. My son, aged twelve, was beaten and tortured in a wood in September, and we've had five court appearances, and it's still going on and it's had a great effect on everybody, and I just wanted maybe to share some of this and work out really how I have coped, which hasn't been very well.

(Liverpool)

I was attacked one afternoon when I was walking my neighbour's dog. I was about a minute from my back door. There's some woodland, and some guy attacked me. He was wearing a balaclava mask, and it was the most awful thing, because you feel all sorts of things like anger and violent thoughts towards the person who attacked you. I was numb for three months ...

(Bristol)

In 1986, John Sentamu's home in London, where he lived with his wife and two children, was set on fire by arsonists. The smoke damage was extensive; the whole of the kitchen was nearly gutted, and had to be redone. The children were at school when it happened, but he and his wife were upstairs in the bedroom:

Soon afterwards a gentleman rang and said, 'I realise you haven't burned in my oven. Next time there will be no opportunity for you to survive. I've left one of the petrol bombs in your garden. If you are clever enough, you'll find it.' So there was a search party and it was discovered by a member of the church.

Two days later, he received a letter through the post, first class, smeared with human excreta:

The language was just unbelievable; there was a lot of hate. The letter said I was black, and should not be the vicar of that parish, and the area belonged to this particular gentleman, who claimed he had every right to own it. Because we had just fostered two extra children, he also said 'You are breeding like rats, and we do not want an increase in population in black people.' And that's why the gentleman did it.

The family's response was not to move, but to stick it out:

We felt as a family, plus the two children we had just fostered, that we would not leave the smell. We will stay with the stink in this particular house until it was put right, and live through it. And as a family we lived and cooked in one room for about eight weeks, until the house was sorted out; and as the house was slowly being brought back to normality, you felt that as the smell of the smoke was disappearing, your anger was also going at the same time. So it was a very cleansing experience.

To this day, the police have never found the arsonist.

John Sentamu also experienced violence in Uganda. In 1973, during the regime of General Idi Amin, he was arrested and imprisoned. A magistrate himself, he was beaten up in gaol by Amin's soldiers. So what helped him through?

First, I found myself saying words like these: 'You may destroy this body, which after all, one day will die, but John Sentamu you are not going to get hold of, because he is loved by his family, he is loved by God, he is loved by everyone.' So there was this sheer defiance: 'You will not break me.' And that's how I managed.

He had also memorised many psalms, and found himself reciting particularly those psalms full of anger, and fantasising about the people responsible for his imprisonment and mistreatment.

I think we've all got fantasies. You get these particularly in the psalms, where the psalmist prays his prayers, and wants the kids of his enemies to be blown out and turned into slime. But the amazing thing is, because he's fantasising about that, he doesn't actually cause any harm. And towards the end, he's actually praising God.

One of the things he discovered from the psalms was the need not to sit upon fantasies and very deep emotions, but to release them, and find God in them:

Instead of simply disowning them, or trying to suppress them, they should be expressed. And once they're expressed, with the light of God, they may actually be brought into proper perspective. Anger, to me, is a natural expression of self-preservation. If there wasn't that, there would be no reality at all. It actually helped me, and that's why for me, bottled anger doesn't exist.

2 Fear of Anger

Many Christians have been taught that anger is an unacceptable feeling, unsuitable for the Christian ideals of serenity and graciousness, and damaging and destructive in its effect on others. One listener described how his life had been clouded by a recurrent difficulty in coping with anger—both his own and other people's:

Another person's anger can flatten me and create a barrier in that relationship, perhaps for years. I feel I am vulnerable to that person: they have a power which they can use against me, and I don't have that. Some years ago, an outburst from a colleague triggered a near-breakdown and depression, which took me months to recover from. All because the colleague was angry with something I had written!

No doubt I have anger inside me, but I rarely get angry ... This puts me in Catch 22 dilemma: if I contain my anger, it can become an oppressive burden. If I let my anger out, I feel guilty. Something in me says: 'How can you be a Christian, yet direct your destructive or hurtful anger at someone else?'

In an interview on Radio 4 in the programme *In the Psychiatrist's Chair*, the journalist Paul Johnson once said: 'People are not afraid of anger, but they are afraid of the irrationality that goes with it.' Two Ugandan proverbs make a similar point:

Act nothing in furious passion: it is putting to sea in a storm.

You can't always be hitting the ceiling without making people think there is something wrong upstairs.

Fear of the irrationality that so often accompanies outbursts of anger may be one reason why anger usually features high in St Paul's disapproving lists of unchristian behaviour. The impression is of anger being permitted only when a cause is 'righteous' and when our feelings are quite uncomplicated by self-interest (whenever that rare situation might be). Yet the texts themselves throw a slightly different light: 'In your anger, do not sin: do not let the sun go down while you are still angry' (Ephesians 4.26 NIV); or 'Love is not easily angered' (1 Corinthians 13.5 NIV). These are not saying that love is *never* angry. So why do so many people feel there is a total religious taboo on anger?

To John Sentamu, this idea of a taboo implies a very strange view of God—a God that, in his book, does not exist. Lionel agreed. The Bible, he said, is full of anger:

God is angry with the children of Israel, the children of Israel are angry with each other, the prophets are angry with the children of Israel, the children have some pretty nasty thoughts about them. And of course in the New Testament too, Jesus is angry with his disciples, Jesus curses the fig tree, there's an awful lot of anger going round, and the thing I don't understand, considering there's so much anger in the Bible from everybody, is why modern religion tries to be so angerless.

So, it was back to the Bible, to Exodus 32.19-20. Moses has received the ten commandments on Mount Sinai. He descends to the Israelite camp, to find them worshipping not God, but a golden bull calf, a symbol of all the idolatry of greed, gold, and materialism that has plagued the world before and since:

When Moses came close enough to the camp to see the bull-calf and to see the people dancing, he was furious. There at the foot of the mountain, he threw down the tablets he was carrying and broke them. He took the bull-

calf, which they had made, melted it, ground it into fine powder, and mixed it with water. Then he made the people of Israel drink it.

(Good News Bible)

Jesus of Nazareth gets angry too:

[Jesus] went into the temple and began driving out those who bought and sold in the temple. He upset the tables of the money-changers and the seats of the dealers in pigeons; and he would not allow anyone to use the temple court as a thoroughfare for carrying goods. Then he began to teach them, and said, 'Does not Scripture say, "My house shall be called a house of prayer for all the nations"? But you have made it a robbers' cave.'

Mark 11. 15–17 (NEB)

To John Sentamu, the temple in Jerusalem was a place where everybody, regardless of their status, should come and freely worship:

Yet some were trying to marginalise other people, and put them in a corner. So the anger there of Jesus is of one who feels 'Yes, I do love humanity, but I really am angry at the inhumanity I'm experiencing.' I think that anger is one of the sinews of being human, and you can't run away from it.

But what about the danger of just anger slipping into self-righteous anger? In ourselves, how do we tell one from another there? 'Self-righteous anger is phoney anger,' said Lionel Blue.

It's when you're trying to hoick up the anger inside you, to boost it, put on the amplifiers; when there's something rather false in it; when you're enjoying your anger; and when you're using it for political purposes; when behind all the emotion, there's something cold, calculating, directing it. That's what I object to.

Anger is energy, coiled up inside us; and if you try and censor out that energy, you lose any capacity to reform things, to change things, to do anything in the world. The rabbis once said 'Why did God create the evil inclination?'—and I suppose that anger is part of the evil inclination—and they said 'Without the evil inclination, people wouldn't build cities, have civilisation and create things at all.' Anger is one of the great engines inside us, provided we can control it, and it doesn't control us.

But *how* do we control it? After all, anger is often triggered when we feel insecure, threatened, trapped, vulnerable, or depressed. A Hasidic story tells how one famous rabbi, Rabbi Mendel, was accustomed to restrain an angry rebuke until he had investigated a list of many hundreds of commands to learn whether anger was permissible in this particular instance. The question was: how much genuine anger could he feel after completing his search?

Shall men, then, always walk in meekness? Not so, say the Masters. There are moments when haughtiness becomes a duty. When the Evil Inclination approaches, whispering in the ear: 'You are unworthy to fulfil the Law,' say 'I am worthy.'

3 Anger at Poverty and Unemployment

I am black born in South Africa, married to a born and bred English man. My husband got a newspaper managing job in Saltash, with a flat above the shop. They were happy with my husband's performance. But as soon as the mother of the shop owner noticed that I was black, there was an immediate dismissal.

(Plymouth)

As a skilled professional I found that registering as an unemployed person made me a non-person, a person not to be believed, a person who would cheat if they could, a person not worth anything, so my skills are worth nothing, any job would do for me. I had to cope with the anxiety about money ... I have to be available for work at very short notice and find my own transport. I couldn't plan, I couldn't hope, and I had to face the contempt of other people because I was unemployed. A situation like this requires justice. My God is a

God of justice. Apparently he is absent and silent here. Those who have devised a policy of high unemployment are in desperate spiritual danger.

(North Yorkshire, woman)

———

During Lionel Blue's childhood in London's East End in the 1930s, what really soured him, he says now, was being the object of pity, of charity. The only job his father could get during the Depression was selling ice-cream in the winter: 'He used to give me an ice-cream, and I used to smile. But I used to think "My God, they're murdering him, they're taking away his dignity, they're ruining him." Beneath that smile I was very angry indeed.'

That fuelled all the marches and politics he went into, years later. One temporary escape route, as a child, was fantasising about being rich:

> I went into all the fantasies of being a changeling, of really being the child of rich, noble parents and how one day, I'd come into my own—all that kind of thing, which children do. I used to tell the other children that I had a house with two gable fronts and so many windows; and of course it was just a completely ordinary house. But I found it somehow was already destroying my self-confidence; and I think that's one thing I went to religion for—because it was the one place where I didn't really have to act, where I could be me as I was actually was.

John Sentamu's childhood in Uganda was even poorer—he was one of thirteen children. He was about eighteen before he got his first pair of shoes, and all the clothes were handed down from one child in the family to another. But his experience was the exact opposite to Lionel's:

> I didn't feel like Lionel, because I suppose in the village where we grew up, we were all nearly at the same level. Nobody was richer than we were, and in fact because my parents were teachers, we were slightly better maybe than others, but not in material terms. We all felt we belonged to

a community, an extended family. I think that's what helped me. But coming to this country and then finding people who had far more material wealth, and yet grumbling, and not being thankful, not being grateful, I said to myself, 'They should come to live in Uganda in a little village, and see what it is like.'

Lionel responded that if his parents had let him just be an ordinary East End kid, there would have been no emotional problem. 'It was precisely because they wanted to get me out of it, which alienated me from my surroundings, that all the anger came.'

Lionel's anger may well have spurred him on to do and become what he has become. Stevie Smith's poem, *Anger's Freeing Power*, explores the paradox that anger can sometimes be a more effective force for change and liberation than love. The poem describes a dream she had of a much-loved pet raven 'imprisoned' in a room with only three walls. She pleads with it to realise it has 'made a prison of a place that is not one at all', and encourages it to fly free through the open wall. But it cannot see its freedom until two fellow ravens make it angry, by mocking its stupidity; only then does the bird escape its prison:

And in my dream I watched him go
And I was glad, I loved him so.

Yet when I woke my eyes were wet
To think Love had not freed my pet.

Anger it was that won him hence
As only Anger taught him sense.

Often my tears fall in a shower
Because of Anger's freeing power.

4 Anger at Being Rejected—at Work

In 1979, my health authority began a formal investigation into criticism of my work by two of my medical colleagues. Ten years later I was declared redundant. The year after that, an industrial tribunal showed I had been wrongfully dismissed, but I was not allowed to return to work. There has been no diminution in my intense indignation at the appalling injustice

**affecting not only me, but also other innocent doctors. I have
been helped by knowing that God is absolutely just and he
knows my work was not unsatisfactory.**

This was one of many letters from listeners, describing their
anger at personal rejection or injustice by colleagues, friends, or
family. Many letter-writers spoke of faith helping them through,
among them a former schoolteacher. Yet his anger and grief still
obsess him, following a nervous breakdown after a long conflict
with a colleague. He cannot forgive this woman who, he believes, ruined his career:

**I spent fifteen months crying, on sick and disability pay, until
finally receiving my pension on health grounds. Right up to the
present time, if I am under stress, my dreams are of that
woman, rather than any current events ... One of the things I
may do in the next few years is to take a lay reader's course.
However there is one problem which obsesses me. It's
summarised in Matthew 5.23–4:**

*If, when you are bringing your gift to the altar, you
suddenly remember that your brother or sister has a
grievance against you, leave your gift where it is before
the altar. First go and make your peace with your
brother or sister, and only then come back and offer
your gift.*

**I haven't begun to forgive Mrs X, and worse, I don't think I
even want to. What do I do?**

Lionel Blue responded:

There are lots of ways to deal with your anger. He could put
a cushion in a chair, and say it was that woman, and then
shout and scream at it. That's one way of getting rid of it.
Another way is by painting it out. You can also write about
it. You can also join a cause which campaigns against the
injustice.

He personally used sometimes to buy cheap china in charity
shops and smash it against the wall:

Unfortunately china in charity shops has now gone up like everything else, and you can't do that sort of thing! You can write a letter about it, or you can scream and shout and roll on the floor about it, but it's much better out than in, dear, as an old governess used to tell me.

He laughed about the memory, but told us no more about the old governess. The problem, for himself, he went on, had been admitting his own anger in the first place:

Religious people find it quite easy to say, 'Oh, I'm weak, I'm powerless, I'm the victim of injustice, I'm all that sort of thing'; but it's very, very difficult, if you're a religious person, to say you're the angry one. I've been in therapy and analysis for years, and it's taken me years and years to admit that the anger was in me, that I was the one who was angry.

The monks of a neighbouring monastery asked the Master's help in a quarrel that had risen among them. They had heard the Master say he had a technique guaranteed to bring love and harmony to any group.

On this occasion, he revealed it: 'Any time you are with anyone or think of anyone, you must say to yourself: 'I am dying and this person is dying', attempting the while to experience the truth of the words you are saying. If everyone of you agrees to practise this, bitterness will die out, harmony will arise.'

5 Anger at Being Rejected—at Home

I'll never forget the day I heard my brother aged 27 had killed himself. It was a bright sunny October day, with the leaves swirling about in the garden. I was so angry. How could he have done it? What about us—me, my mother and his children too. Didn't he care about any of us? How selfish of him.

That Nottinghamshire letter-writer went on to say that, since her brother's suicide, God's love has helped her through a series of difficulties. But the hurt and anger of feeling rejected by people we love or admire is among the most painful of all human experiences—and the most ancient. Cain murders his brother Abel (Genesis 4) out of anger and jealousy that God accepts Abel and his offering with favour, but rejects his own. Similarly, Jacob's elder sons are filled with anger and jealousy at his preference for their younger brother, Joseph:

> *When Joseph was a boy of seventeen, he used to*
> *accompany his brothers, the sons of Bilhah and Zilpah,*
> *his father's wives, when they were in charge of the flock;*
> *and he brought their father a bad report of them. Now*
> *Israel loved Joseph more than any other of his sons,*
> *because he was a child of his old age, and he made him a*
> *long, sleeved robe. When his brothers saw that their father*
> *loved him more than any of them, they hated him and*
> *could not say a kind word to him.*
>
> Genesis 37.2–4 (NEB)

Soon afterwards, Joseph's brothers get shot of him (temporarily) by selling him for twenty pieces of silver to Midianite merchants on their way to Egypt. They tell their father that a wild beast has devoured him.

As a prison chaplain, John Sentamu came across a number of youngsters hurt by their fathers:

One Sunday I was preaching about God being a loving father, and this young man was getting angry and agitated, and he said 'Come and see me in my prison cell, please.' I went there, he took off his shirt, and he said, 'You talk about God being a loving father', and his back had all been lacerated from beatings of nearly nine years. I had to find a new way of talking about God, so I said, 'Richard, God is a friend who will not grass on you.' I think the only way we can help people is to find a new way of speaking and dealing with their anger; platitudes and statements that don't work won't help them.

In many families, anger is provoked by the pressure of expectations—of how successful children are at school, at work, or socially—by resentment by children or parents at the restraints caused by the other on their freedom of thought and action, by unrelieved insecurity at times of stress. Most families have experienced walk-outs and phones slammed down, followed by reconciliation—tears, and requests for forgiveness. It may even be unhealthy to live without the occasional spat. If we are lucky, a friend or member of our family may have the brilliant knack of puncturing our anger by humour or a gentle word, so that it vanishes in a few seconds. But what if the pattern of rowing carries on in the same old well-worn treadmill, year after year?

Maybe it should be question time. Why do we all keep on behaving like this? Are we giving our families the backwash of anger caused by others (either currently or long ago)? What am I doing personally that provokes, or threatens, or traps? Why do I feel so threatened? Is it worth trying to explain this? How did this pattern start? Would it help if I refused to compete or to rival? What about a temporary ban on negative, hurtful remarks? Would some quiet honest reflection or prayer help?

Among the most painful situations described by listeners was the long slow breakup of their marriage. The husband of one London listener had been trying for as long as eleven months to make up his mind whether he should leave to live with another woman:

> One day she telephoned me to taunt me saying that I had missed my chance, and that she had won. It was an incredible call, leaving me almost gasping with anger, jealousy and frustration. I remember flinging myself down near the foot of my bed. There were no words—just this dreadful, loathsome feeling. Somehow I must have turned to Jesus in that climax of anguish. Suddenly those feelings vanished to be replaced by the most amazing sense of joy—a joy I had never before experienced.
>
> It was truly astonishing—even to me at the time. I *knew* that nothing I could have done or thought could have taken that extremity of pain away, let alone replaced it by such a sense of rightness and joy. It convinced me of the reality of God that he does hear us and has taken on himself our pain.

That listener writes that she is now reconciled to her husband

and his new wife, and regards them as friends; but in many breakups the anger can last for years. Lionel Blue had a relationship that went on for twenty years:

> And I suddenly knew it was over. I remember sitting and thinking, and a voice said inside me, 'Look, don't you realise that all the love in this world is only a reflection of the real love that you'll eventually get (I presume at the moment of death), when you finally meet the being you're praying to, face to face.'

He got back to London, and was soon in a row with his friend:

> We were quarrelling over every pot and every pan, and who owned it, because these were symbols of our anger with each other, and that voice I'd heard suddenly went into my friend, out of my friend, into my friend, out of my friend. It said, 'Can't you see me?' And suddenly I burst into laughter, and said 'Look, let's go to a pub, and toss a coin for everything.' Since then, we've stayed good friends, still fond of each other and affectionate. But that's what happens. When you let God into your anger, the strange thing is it can turn that energy inside out.

> *If one abuses you, there is a temptation to answer back, or to be revenged. One should be on guard against this natural reaction. It is like spitting against the wind, it harms no one but oneself. It is like sweeping dust against the wind, it does not get rid of the dust but defiles oneself. Misfortune always dogs the steps of one who gives way to the desire for revenge.*
>
> (The Teaching of Buddha)

6 Anger and the Passion Story

> *It was nine in the morning when they crucified him; and the inscription giving the charge against him read, 'The King of the Jews'. Two robbers were crucified with him, one on his right and the other on his left. The passers-by wagged their heads and jeered at him: 'Bravo!' they cried, 'So you are the man who was to pull down the temple, and rebuild it in three days! Save yourself and come down from the cross.' The chief priests and scribes joined in,*

*jesting with one another: 'He saved others,' they said, 'but
he cannot save himself. Let the Messiah, the king of Israel,
come down now from the cross. If we see that, we shall
believe.' Even those who were crucified with him taunted
him.*

Mark 15.25–32 (Revised English Bible)

Look at the Passion story, and anger is there: the anger of Jesus
that the Temple, the holy place of God, had been made a den of
thieves; the anger of his enemies, who realised that if his message of love were to be lived out, it would challenge all they held
dear—wealth, power, the religious and social status quo; and the
anger of his friends at his crucifixion.

Over the centuries, ignoring the fact that all the disciples,
Mary and Joseph and Jesus himself were themselves all Jewish,
Christians increasingly heaped the blame and guilt for the crucifixion on the entire Jewish race, past and present. So the Jews
have had a long time to get used to unjust violence and persecution—two thousand years or so. Rarely able to express their
anger publicly without provoking more persecution, they have
had to bottle it up. To Lionel Blue, anger trapped inside can
become a kind of poison:

So Jews have had to find a way of living with anger they
can't express. One of the ways they cope with it is by
humour, because humour can evaporate anger. The other
way Jews have coped with anger is often by thinking of
themselves as weak, powerless, you know, the typical fall
guy, but that doesn't do any good either.

Today, Lionel Blue says a part of him goes along with the whole
Passion story and feels it.

But there's another part of me that remembers I was also the
only Jewish child at a non-Jewish school during the war,
and then it gets very dicey indeed, because you become the
deicide, the Christ-killer, and all that sort of thing. Okay, the
Jews take part in the whole crucifixion story; so do the
Gentiles, with the Romans; but you do find a tendency in
the Gospels gradually to demonise the Jews. First of all,
there's just a crowd, then the crowd in another Gospel
becomes the Jews, and then you find that the mocking of

Jesus by the Roman soldiers then gets attributed to 'they', which presumably means the Jews again. And it's very, very uncomfortable. It's got much better now, but occasionally you still find churches where all the ancient reproaches against the Jews in the liturgy are still retained.

He likes going along to Christmas services, but like most Jews, keeps well out of church at Easter, because neither the congregation, nor he, nor the minister, can handle it.

7 Anger at God

Don't tell me of a faith that fears
To face the world around;
Don't dull my mind with easy thoughts
Of grace without a ground.

I need to know that God is real!
I need to know that Christ can feel
The need to touch and love and heal
The world, including me!

Don't speak of piety and prayers
Absolved from human need;
Don't talk of spirit without flesh
Like harvest without seed.

I need to know that God is real!
I need to know that Christ can feel
The need to touch and love and heal
The world, including me!

(A protest song from the Iona Community,
about bogus religion)

I have severe arthritis. I once watched a programme in which an American TV evangelist stated that lack of faith was the reason for continued illness or disability. The statement worried me, confused me, and made me feel deep anger.

That Harrogate listener's letter stirred in me a professional memory I had long put aside. When I was the BBC religious affairs correspondent, it was part of my job to keep cool, and be fair, whatever interviewees were saying. But on one occasion, I had a little local difficulty. A priest with an influential ministry at that time in the so-called 'charismatic' movement had claimed that, in response to prayer, a tiny example of God's loving care meant that, in an aeroplane, he had been offered a particular fruit juice he liked rather than the standard variety. I had just got back from Africa, so I asked, if God really worked like that, why He was allowing Africans I knew to suffer through famine. His response, in essence, was that the Africans were not praying sincerely enough. When I heard this, my heart felt as if it were pounding out of my body. I had the greatest difficulty controlling my trembling voice to continue.

What so angered me was not just the insulting racism, the deep complacency, or the intellectual crassness, but the huge insult to God. I felt he was propagating a god who was a monster—a god with whom his converts, if they thought about it deeply, would all too easily end up disillusioned and angry.

A number of letters spoke of anger with various images of God they had once, or still, believed in:

Since her death, I felt very angry about losing my friend Daphne and wanted to be angry with God. How could I say that God was omnipotent and then spend all my time excusing him from responsibility in this event that had shattered my life?

That Berkshire listener managed to keep up some conversation with God:

Eventually I realised that what was important was that I didn't try to hide my feelings from Him. He could cope with my anger and fear so that there was no need for them to become a barrier between myself and Him.

But a listener from Liverpool, struck by illness, was so angry that she did not pray for years. A successful, lively former teacher, she has suffered a desperate series of medical disasters, including cancer and a stroke. She has endured it for sixteen years. She has fought to cope on her own with feelings of resentment, panic, anger, despair, and grief for the person she once was.

I was brought up in a truly Christian home, where the 'old values' were absorbed unthinkingly—I never thought of questioning. The stroke destroyed my simple faith and made me think—something I should have done years before. I never once asked 'Why me?'—why not me? I accepted the situation, but I could not believe any more in the Creed. I was surprised my faith was so shallow, but the Bishop of Durham has been a comfort to me—if he questions, why shouldn't I?

For some years she could not pray:

I had to work through my feelings of panic, anger, grief for the person I once was, resentment, despair. Church people, friends and neighbours have been very supportive, but I feel such a burden on others, and I think along the lines of Milton in his ode *On his blindness*:.

> When I consider how my light is spent,
> Ere half my days, in this dark world and wide,
> And that one talent which is death to hide
> Lodged with me useless, though my soul more bent
> To serve therewith my Maker, and present
> My true account, lest he returning chide,
> 'Doth God exact day-labour, light denied?'
> I fondly ask. But Patience, to prevent
> That murmur, soon replies: 'God doth not need
> Either man's work or his own gifts; who best
> Bear his mild yoke, they serve him best. His state
> Is kingly: thousands at his bidding speed,
> And post o'er land and ocean without rest;
> They also serve who only stand and wait.

I reckon I have at last grown up in religious thought. I cannot believe that God is a loving Father. I don't believe in God now at all—just a creator of the Universe, and I certainly don't think that Jesus is the *only* path to salvation. The five great faiths all have great truths at the heart and the believers are good people. The fanatics in all of them are spoiling people's attitude and making them cynical ... Now I just get on with my life day by day and am grateful when I have a happy one.

The day John Sentamu received results from Cambridge University that he had got his doctorate was the same day he received a medical test that he had a terrible blood disorder and needed to have treatment which went on for nearly nine years:

> Every time I went to the clinic, I kept saying 'God, why me? Why don't you take this pain somewhere else?' And as soon as that was just over, my mother came to this country dying of cancer, and she really died a most painful death. And I remember going to God, and saying, 'If I could see you face to face, God, I would spit at you and tell you what I think.' And I remember suddenly a little voice saying, 'But you'd be spitting at yourself, because I'm all around you, I'm all surrounding you.' Oh yes, I've screamed, I've shouted.

Lionel too has felt something of the same anger as John. He was staying behind in a church once, when some friends went to see the site of a concentration camp:

> I couldn't cope with it; and when I was in that church, I said to God, 'Why the hell didn't you take a hand in it?' But then I thought, 'Well, God hasn't got any hands, so he's useless.' And I prowled round that church, not knowing what to do, but as I went out of the gate, something hit me. It said, '*You're* his hands. And your anger with God, "Why doesn't he take a hand in it?", is really saying "Why don't *you* take a hand in it?", because you're the only hands he's got in the world.'

Buddha to bandit:
'... It is you who are crazy to think that you are mighty because you can wound and destroy. That is the task of children. The mighty know how to create and heal ...'

My nineteen-year-old daughter was killed in the Lockerbie air disaster. She was a passenger on the Pan Am plane that was

blown out of the sky. Five days after her death, I sat at her desk, and the last verse of Romans chapter 12 came to my mind 'Don't be overcome by evil, but overcome evil by doing good.' I was struggling with the attitude of some other family members, a lot of families who were wanting to strike back, to hit back and feeling that if we hit back at others in the way that they hit at us we make ourselves no better than they are, and we give the devil one hundred per cent interest on his investment ... That verse came to me 'overcome evil by doing good' and really we've discovered it's the only possible way to win ... We've built a children's home in the Philippines with gifts given by kind friends, we have helped other organisations a little bit and we've seen a lot of good come through our efforts.

———

On a street I saw a naked child, hungry and shivering in the cold. I became angry and said to God, 'Why do you allow this? Why don't you do something?'

God did not reply. That night he said, quite suddenly, 'I certainly did something. I made you.'

(Anthony de Mello)

Meditation

Calm me, O Lord, as you stilled the storm
Still me, O Lord, keep me from harm:
Let all tumult cease,
Enfold me, Lord, in your peace.

(David Adam)

———

Let us bring to mind:

all that has spoken most directly to us.

We bring to mind

those angry at injustice ...
those angry at being rejected ...
all those angry with God.

We bring to mind too

any anger and violence in our own homes or place of work ...
the anger within ourselves ...
and its effects on our own lives and the lives of others.

Come, God.
Come with the angry
Come with the rejected
Come with the powerless
Come with those who long for something better,
Come and lead us to where you are living
and show us what you want us to do.

* * * * * * * *

(Music)

* * * * * * * *

Loving Lord,
who grieves over
all the violence of the world,
give us courage to voice our deepest feelings
we lay open to you:
the wounds that have misshaped our lives;
the injuries we cannot forget and have not forgiven.

Forgive us
for the wounds we have inflicted;
the injuries we cannot forget and for which we have not been
forgiven.

We pray for all victims of violent anger
all who are brutalised or neglected
insulted or threatened.

And for all those in the grip of anger ...

(You could pray your own prayers here—perhaps mention those
we ourselves have angered, those who have angered us, those
angry in the news. This is what Lionel, John and I thought of:)

Lionel: I think of the people in AIDS wards ...

John: I think of the prisoners, their victims, those who face
unjust trials, unjust treatment ...

John: I think of those many refugees, no roof over their head,
hungry, frustrated, frightened ...

Lionel: I think of all those occupied by foreign powers and for
what they must feel ...

Rosemary: And for torturers, that they will see the horror of what
they do, and be changed ...

Lionel: I think of the muggers themselves as well as their victims, and all terrorists.

You are home to the exile
touch to the frozen
daylight to the prisoner
authority to the silent
anger to the helpless
laughter to the weary
direction to the joyful:
come, our God, come.

(Janet Morley)

* * * * * * * * *

(Song)

* * * * * * * * *

St Paul wrote:
Each of you must put off falsehood and speak truthfully to
his neighbour, for we are all members of one body. 'In your
anger, do not sin': Do not let the sun go down while you
are still angry, and do not give the devil a foothold ... Get
rid of all bitterness, rage and anger, brawling and slander,
along with every form of malice. Be kind and
compassionate to one another, forgiving each other, just as
in Christ God forgave you.
                                    Ephesians 4.25–27; 31–32 (NIV)

Lord, help me to acknowledge the anger inside me, which fright-
ens me, because it sometimes threatens to overwhelm me. Give
me the humour and humility to recognise that it's there, and that
it's mine. Give me the courage not to hide it, but to use it, not to
hurt others, but to help them. And may it also help me, to speak
out against cruelty and injustice, to state the unwelcome truth,
and to understand the anger of others. O Lord, help me transform
my anger so that I can make it useful.

(Lionel Blue)

* * * * * * * * *

(Song)

* * * * * * * * *

Isaiah said:
The wolf also shall dwell with the lamb, and the leopard
shall lie down with the kid; and the calf and the young
lion and the fatling together; and a little child shall lead
them. And the cow and the bear shall feed; their young
ones shall lie down together: and the lion shall eat straw
like the ox. And the sucking child shall play on the hole of
the asp, and the weaned child shall put his hand on the
cockatrice' den. They shall not hurt nor destroy in all my
holy mountain: for the earth shall be full of the knowledge
of the Lord, as the waters cover the sea.

Isaiah 11.6–9 (AV)

May the Winds, the Oceans,
The Herbs, the Nights and the Days,
The Mother Earth,
The Father Heaven,
All Vegetation, the Sun,
Be all sweet to us.

Let us follow the path of Goodness
For all times, like the Sun and the Moon
Moving eternally in the Sky.
Let us be charitable to one another.
Let us not kill or be violent with one another.
Let us know and appreciate the points of view of others
And let us unite.
May the God who is friendly,
Benevolent, all-encompassing, measurer of everything
The Sovereign, the Lord of Speech,
May he shower his blessings on us.
Oh Lord, remove my indiscretion and arrogance,
Control my Mind.
Put an end to the snare of Endless Desire. Amen.

(From an old Hindu prayer)

* * * * * * * *

(Music)

* * * * * * * * * *

Some Suggestions for Worship Music

1 *St John Passion*, by J. S. Bach.
2 'Aus Liebe will mein Heiland sterben' from *St Matthew Passion*, by J. S. Bach.
3 Song: 'When from the darkness comes no light' by Colin Mawby/Brendan McLaughlin, from *Worship Songs Ancient and Modern no 95* (Faber).
4 'The Sorrow' (tune: Reality) by John Bell (Iona Community).
5 'A Gaelic Blessing' from CD *Gloria—the Sacred Music of John Rutter*, (RSCM/Collegium Records).

Other Music

6 'The World is Mean' by Bertolt Brecht and Kurt Weill, from LP *The Threepenny Opera* (Polydor).
7 'Dies Irae' by Verdi, from *The Requiem*.

SYLVIA SANDS is a peace worker. She lives in East Belfast, and works in the Northern Ireland Hospice, the Royal Victoria Hospital, in peace communities and with OASIS, a group for marginalised people.

After several years of being involved ecumenically with churches in England, for ten years she worked in Belfast with 'Compass', a peace group which brought together Catholic and Protestant young people, during one of the most violent decades of the 'troubles'.

In 1981, she moved to the Blue Stack mountains of County Donegal, running a hermitage-retreat specially for people bereaved or affected by the violence in Belfast.

Returning to Belfast in 1987, she lived on the peace line up the Shankill Road, sharing the tensions of the huge wall that divides the city. She has written two books.

ROY MCCLELLAND has, since 1985, been Professor of Mental Health at Queen's University, Belfast. He is a Fellow and sub-dean of the Royal College of Psychiatrists. His research has included studies of head injury, schizophrenia, childhood autism, dyslexia, hearing impairment and electroconvulsive therapy.

For the past seventeen years, he has been deeply involved in the medical and psychiatric training of undergraduates and postgraduates, with special responsibility for undergraduate programmes on interviewing and counselling, leadership and team work, and medical ethics. Among his many other professional commitments he was, in 1993 and 1994, visiting professor at the University of Buenos Aires.

He is a member of the Corrymeela Community, a Christian group that works for reconciliation in Northern Ireland.

FOUR

Disappointment

There was once a king who had a beautiful diamond, and he was very proud of it because it was unique. But one day the diamond got deeply scratched and nobody could remove the scratch or repair the fault, and the king was very sad. Then a jeweller came who said he could make the diamond even better than it was before. The king doubted him at first, but then entrusted him with the stone. And when the workman had finished, the king saw that he had engraved round the flaw a lovely rosebud, and the ugly scratch had become the stem.

———

Having a thing of beauty damaged is a universal experience. It may be a jewel, a hope, a relationship, an ambition. Yet that old Jewish story suggests that even the greatest disappointment, the most damaged relationship, can be changed into something better. The ancient Chinese philosopher, Confucius, put it like this: 'The gem cannot be polished without friction.' The problem for many who wrote in, or phoned, was how to live through this friction and disappointment—whether disappointment in career ambitions and material hopes, in broken family relationships, disappointment in God or the Church, in friends, or just in life in general:

After going out with a bloke whom I loved very much for three years, believing that God had put us together and we would marry, he told me that he did not wish to get married—in his words, as an airline pilot, he 'had the world at his feet and did not wish to be tied down'. I wanted to die.

(Lancaster)

My feelings as I reach my mid-sixties are profound disappointment and frustration in not having fulfilled anything in life. In the film *Shirley Valentine*, one of the lines runs 'We lead such little lives.' I feel that could be said of me, and I cried within myself 'But it shouldn't have been like that.'

(Hull)

My mother and I came to live in this town twenty years ago. I was really unhappy in my new job, such a contrast to a previous one where I'd felt perfectly competent. After five years work, I quit the profession. I have tried other work, without success. So I am long-term unemployed.

(Lancashire)

I felt like a child peering through a shop window, and not allowed to have anything I wanted.

(Hertfordshire)

———

Of all occupations, peace work in Northern Ireland has been, in the past, one of the most prone to disappointment (as well as to satisfaction). For over twenty years, Sylvia Sands has been committed to this, helping to rebuild lives destroyed or hurt by what has happened there. She now works for OASIS—a group which backs people who feel on the very edges of society in Belfast. Yet her deepest disappointment was a personal disappointment, when she lost her marriage, her home, and her vocation. She and her husband had set up a hermitage-retreat in County Donegal for people bereaved or affected by the violence in Belfast. This worked magically for retreatants; but her marriage hit the rocks. She felt a bit like Miss Haversham in Dickens's *Great Expectations*—covered in cobwebs: 'There's a bitterness about disappointment—the iron enters your soul; but it was important to feel it was a passage, a tunnel through which I would travel rather than the place where I would live.'

And it has been.

As a professor of mental health, Roy McClelland has faced daily serious psychiatric problems like schizophrenia and autism in patients; so he might be expected to regard mere disappointment as a relatively minor experience. Minor or not, he certainly regards it as very common. Indeed, the only guaranteed way to avoid all disappointment would be to have absolutely no hopes, no ambitions, no expectations. 'It doesn't matter which side of the consultation you're on. Psychiatrists are not protected, and I've experienced disappointment like everybody else.'

He reckons that beneath the lid of the catch-all word 'disappointment' lie a number of feelings—like anger and resentment. It is only when we recognise these feelings as facts, admit to them, and look at them, that we can begin to understand what our disappointment and unfulfilled hopes are really about.

One of the hardest areas to be honest with ourselves is over people we love most, and where our failed hopes and dreams wound deepest—our families:

1 Disappointment in Children

My daughter was arrested and given a fourteen-year jail sentence. She was only 21 at the time. [You can imagine] the shock and the heartache and the problems that arose out of that. My husband is a priest in a remote part of Wales, and our love for our daughter is very, very great.

Last year, I was told that my son and his wife were splitting up. It came as a complete shock to me. Over the months that followed, bitterness grew between them: in breaking up and selling a home after sixteen (seemingly happy) years; causing disruption and deep upset to two lovely boys; and now of my son living out his life in isolation, and finding consolation in drinking. What a mess it all is for them.

(Ipswich)

The most devastating experience for us was when our beloved younger daughter took her own life violently whilst in her final year as a medical student. It was a heartbreaking time.

(Cornwall)

In the letters about disappointment over families, several complex emotions were often interwoven. Some disappointments and griefs were rooted in tragic external circumstances, like accidents. Others seemed to be rooted, partly at least, in unrealistic expectations—parents wanting children to achieve or outdo their own failed ambitions, unable to accept that the children's own hopes and dreams were different. Sometimes, disappointments arose from a failure to achieve goals which were defined not so much by the individuals themselves as by their peer groups; the fear of what other people would think, and a consequent loss of prestige, were powerful factors in some disappointment. Many parents blamed themselves for the real or perceived failures of their children.

As a child, Sylvia Sands felt she was a disappointment to her parents:

> The pressures on me were not academic, but I was expected to be respectful and normal, like Doris Day in a gingham apron really. I rebelled against that, and became most peculiar, dressed like a French tart, and the only people I had any dealings with for about two or three years were people who had police records. So, I was a deep disappointment to the whole family, I think. And yet I have a feeling I was a scapegoat for the real problem. I was the problem that presented itself to the family, but I think the real underlying problem was my father's drink problem.

Sylvia heard years afterwards that, at one stage, her mother had a series of phone calls from people saying things like, 'Do you know what Sylvia said to me in the bus queue today? Do you know where Sylvia is going now and who she's going with?'

> I heard years later that one day my mother stood up for me, and cut into a tirade of abuse against me, and said, 'Oh, go and eat coke!' and put the phone down. That was a lovely solidarity really, and I wish I'd known at the time about it.

One Worcestershire listener described in a letter her intense grief and disappointment at the death of her much-loved second daughter in a car accident:

She was just eighteen. Her boyfriend was driving. He played

rugby and had been heavily drinking all of Saturday afternoon. After the crash, he left her in the car expecting the ambulance to arrive very quickly, which it did.

He turned up the next day very *sober*, expecting her to be in a recovery ward, not in the morgue. What a shock for him. He went to pieces for days, he didn't eat, etc. His mum kept phoning me, to speak to him.

It was very hard for me to forgive him. I felt no pity for him, but I did for her seeing her child suffering. I wouldn't have wanted my own children to suffer in that way. Many people didn't understand my forgiveness, they said they never could. I was given great strength at that time ... God bless anyone in this situation.

Another listener described her huge disappointment that her son was homosexual, and how she and her husband coped with it, even though they felt able to trust only one friend with their distress:

My world crumbled around me one evening when, after a long hard struggle, my son eventually told my husband and myself, that he was gay. He was just eighteen. One thing was certain, as we had listened to his struggles and seen his distress, we knew this happening had been unwanted and unasked for. Our hearts were overwhelmed with love for him, and we tried, calmly to convey that to him.

A few minutes later, it was all over, he left to go and stay the night with a friend in the next town.

The house seemed strangely silent when he had gone. I was heart-broken, devastated. Adding to my distress was the fact that his room was empty except for boxes filled with his belongings, he had thought we might turn him out.

I couldn't imagine the pain he was going through. I cried and cried. He came home again the next day, and a barrier had gone from between us. He had always been so easy to love,

but now, somehow, there was greater love between us. He just badly needed to know that we loved him, and accepted him, as he was.

For herself, it was as though, she says, a dark cloud had gone over the sun. Who could she turn to for help?

A well-trusted friend put her arm around my shoulders and wept with me. A letter arrived from a support group in answer to my plea. It brought comfort and the assurance of prayer backing. These things greatly helped, but we knew that many of our friends and acquaintances suffered from homophobia, so in order to prevent more pain to ourselves, and our son, we needed to keep things to ourselves.

One Sunday morning, as I arrived at church for worship, the struggle suddenly gripped me. 'How could I worship God, look what he had allowed?' This was my darkest moment. I hesitated, then I remembered how faithful God had been to us in the past. Very gradually our fears were calmed, and a quiet assurance that God had everything in control, filled our hearts.

2 Disappointment in Parents

I was stigmatised with the albatross of illegitimacy. Unfortunately my father who was an RAF pilot killed in the Second World War was unable to fulfil his desire to marry my mother. Since when, I was unrecognised by the RAF, victimised by my mother, and totally ignored by my father's family, who were told by my mother that she had put me in a Salvation Army home ... This problem will never go away, but as I grow older the stigma grows worse.

(North Yorkshire)

A number of letters and calls from listeners described disappointment in their parents. Writing on the ideal relationship between parents and children, St Paul assumes respect and love:

Children, obey your parents, for it is right that you should. 'Honour your father and mother' is the first commandment

with a promise attached, in the words: 'that it may be well
with you and that you may live long in the land'. You
fathers, again, must not goad your children to resentment.
Ephesians 6.1–4 (NEB)

Yet in fact the Bible has many stories where individuals are
goaded into resentment by the behaviour of relatives. Today the
problem remains: how to honour parents who may not be very
honourable?

Roy McClelland reckons that often we put parents on a
pedestal, making them some saintly figure that we choose to follow, and then we discover—surprise, surprise—they are human
like we are. To get past that hurt and disappointment, he empha-
sised how important it is to recognise that our parents too are
often victims of their own histories and early lives. Sylvia Sands
felt that very much about her father:

The extraordinary thing about my relationship with him
was that I was angry with my dad until he died. I wanted
him to be Clint Eastwood, but he became more and more the
kind of person who fell down drunk. But I was always aware
that within my father was always a magnificent man trying
to get out, who got drowned by whisky, and cheap wine.

When he died, she was able to take a step back. It was not so
much that to understand all was to forgive all; instead it was
almost as if she did not need to forgive, because she could see
the reasons why he had turned to the bottle.

I could also see it was an illness, and not just a stigma; so I
felt reconciled to my father. I also realised that to be angry is
to love. I'd always thought I'd hated him, and in actual fact
I realised that indifference is the killer, not anger. So if anyone out there is angry with their parents, I think it means
you love them.

Reflecting on how some of my own behaviour has been affected
by disappointments that go back two or three generations in my
own family, I wondered aloud to Roy McClelland how typical of
many families that would be?

I think most things travel forward, and love travels forward
and hurt travels forward; when we look back as children

towards our parents, we see often that the difficulties they may have visited on us have, in fact, been problems visited on them in their own upbringing.

John Lennon identified this in his song *Mother*, which opens 'Mother you had me, but I never had you. I wanted you, but you didn't want me.' It describes the cycle of being abandoned emotionally by parents, and of following the learned pattern by then abandoning them, and subsequently your own children. The song explores the question of whether, if someone has never been truly loved, he or she can risk loving others. Since no real communication has been experienced or risked for so long, the singer's message to mother, parents, and children is finally just a sad 'Goodbye'.

Sylvia Sands thinks that, as a mother, she passed on to her sons damage she experienced as a daughter. The damage, she thinks, was an atmosphere of denial, a refusal to recognise or admit things that were wrong. Just as her parents denied her father's drink problem, she denied her own marriage difficulties:

> I was then an overtly religious mother, very much involved with the peace movement; and so, when the boys were little, they would come round if I spoke from a pulpit or a platform; and my boys had me right up on a pedestal. Then when the marriage ended, and everything went, I fell off. I didn't just have feet of clay, I had clay right up to the neck! I think my boys were bitterly disappointed because I'd shielded them. I'd pretended in my personal life that everything was all right and that I was one hundred per cent OK; but I was OK as a public figure and desperately not OK as a private person.

For about two or three years, she says, her sons found it difficult even to be with her:

> I set their teeth on edge, because their disappointment was really very deep. But my eldest son came to me with a huge long list one day, and we spent more than a whole day going through his gripes, going through his history from birth right up to the present day; and some things I pleaded guilty to, and other things, I said 'No, "Innocent", I'm innocent of that

charge.' (She laughed). And that was the beginning of a breakthrough—honesty, I think.

To Roy McClelland, anger needs to be accepted back by the parents, 'and then we can start to confront reality. And I hear a little bit of that in Sylvia's story, where some of her son's anger was quite misplaced. We've got to accept we have human parents, just as others of us have human children.'

Rivalry too can be a factor is many family disputes and disappointments. How can that be broken?

The first key step is to recognise that rivalry is real, and envy is very much here to stay; that we are in competition often, sometimes between children and parents, sometimes between children themselves. We need to start talking about it, and to bring out the secret, because often we resist recognising and acknowledging that we are rivalling.

One Dorset listener described the long-term goal as 'forgiveness'. Her mother was a manic depressive, and her own childhood and the years since, she wrote, had been very unhappy because of the emotional and psychological abuse she suffered:

In 1982, my parents were staying with my husband and I for a short holiday. My mother was following me round the house, screaming, and out into the garden in an attempt to control a financial decision concerning our married life. I began to feel ill, and my husband took me out in our car. While he was putting in petrol at a garage, I heard myself say 'Lord, I forgive mother.' I could not believe I had said these words and did not feel I forgave her, but the Lord took me at my word and the process started. My mother died eleven years later, and I was able to tell her many times that I had forgiven her and loved her.

3 Disappointment in Life

The hardest experience to many who wrote in was the sense of being dealt a hand of cards in the game of life, with no aces or royal cards, but mostly twos and threes. We had several moving letters from listeners with disabled children. Rachel has Down's Syndrome. Her mother wrote to describe not only the disappointment of handicap, but the social rejection that followed:

When Rachel was young, pregnant women crossed the road when they saw her, or avoided passing our house. As Rachel grew too old to go into children's group at church, I took her away from the congregation in order not to disturb them during our Rector's excellent sermons. I would have liked somebody to have offered to take her out occasionally so I could listen to a sermon. Twice in the past six months someone has offered to sit with her at home, so that my husband and I could go out. We appreciated this. I'd like someone to invite the three of us into their home to share a meal. When I do have the courage to express our needs, this tends to come out and creates an emotional outburst! This is remembered! Rachel has little language, but is very loving.

Roy McClelland recalled an Irish saying, 'the gift of the handicapped', and said he often had great difficulty in understanding what it meant:

> But I can understand that a home where there's a handicapped child, often has a very different atmosphere from many of our homes where our children are being pushed and groomed for the 11-plus that we still have here in Belfast.

So it's the reverse side of the rivalry and competition?

> Exactly. They are, in a sense, out of the game, and there can be a sense of peace where there are less ambitious objectives for life, where it's about getting along and looking at a child's uncertain future.

Sylvia Sands reckons our society is obsessed with perfection: 'Women, and men too, work hours and hours at getting the body beautiful, and can become absolutely horrible people inside.'

She was loath to say much about handicapped children, because she had not had very much experience of them,

> but it does seem to me we should concentrate on the spirit of the person inside. I have a friend who's the mother of a child with recurring mental illness, as opposed to handicap, and she says that since this has shown up, she's met a better class of parent! She means there's a fellowship, that comes from that kind of stress, that kind of pressure.

I recalled a Christian friend of my own who has a handicapped son. He knows of the danger of setting his own expectations too low, in order to avoid yet more disappointment, as yet again his son is labelled and put near the bottom of the list. He speaks too of how his son's handicap restricts and circumscribes his own life, and exhausts his own style. Before the boy's birth, my friend knew in theory the Christian doctrine that God loves all equally; but when his son was born, he was challenged really to believe it. It led him, he says, to a different understanding of that teaching.

What has most helped Rachel's mother is finding God present in Rachel. She wrote this loving and very personal poem about her, based on Psalm 23, and written during a retreat:

The Lord is my handicapped daughter, Rachel.
She lets me rest within her arms
And leads me into her peace.
Her gentleness, her warmth and her smile of love
Revive me and take away my fear.
As we travel on our journey together
As she gradually deteriorates,
Her ministry of love is always with me.
Wherever her presence has been, is or will be
The pain, the joy and the love of Rachel will always remain.

4 Disappointment in Partnership

I have a girlfriend who I've been going out with for about six or seven years. We used to go everywhere together, no arguments, nothing, and then on Christmas Eve, I took my Christmas present, and she gave me a card saying 'to the one I love', loads of kisses, walked through the door and became a different person, hardly spoken to me since ... When she arranged to see me after Christmas, three times, she never turned up ... it sort of hit me, as you can appreciate, very badly. I've nobody to share it with, I haven't got much of a family.

(Liverpool)

My husband died at the age of 45 after a failed kidney transplant. As we were only married for two years, I felt

**extremely cheated by this short stretch of happiness that life
had handed out to us. In my attempt to suppress the pain of
his death, I've spent quite a lot of money going on foreign
holidays with and without my children, and indulging in many
shopping sprees. However the only release has come through
study—I am now a mature student, reading for a university
degree.**

(Stockport)

A number of letters described the disappointment of broken relationships. Sylvia Sands lost everything after the breakup of her
marriage.

I lost my husband, my home, my children (though they'd
flown the nest by then anyway). I ended up homeless and on
the brew (on the dole) in Belfast. It was the lowest point in
my life. I was desperately disappointed in everything.

But then, astonishingly, came what she calls the liberation of
failure:

I think failure can be a liberating thing, because I was left
with the possibility of finding out who I really am, and what
I really want to do. There's that song 'Freedom's just another word for nothing left to lose', and there's a liberation in
failure where you stop asking the wrong things of yourself.
I think sometimes disappointment comes when we simply
ask the wrong things of ourselves.

Maybe that was what the nineteenth-century American thinker
and writer, Emerson, meant when he wrote: 'Beware of what you
want for you will get it.' Or Jean Ingelow: 'I have lived to thank
God that all my prayers have not been answered.' Or Oscar
Wilde: 'There are two great tragedies in life: one is never getting
what you want and the other is getting exactly what you want.'
People can plot and work and pray for a goal, only for it to turn
to ashes in the end. It is then, says Roy McClelland, that (para-
doxically) disappointment offers opportunities. 'It's not until
you're on the down side of the game, that you realise that much
of what we're into is merely games of one sort of another, and not
about reality and the true stuff of life, which is relationships.'
    The process of taking up these new opportunities and insights

may involve accepting that an earlier chapter in our lives has now closed:

Once there was a young woman called Kisagotami, the wife of a wealthy man, who lost her mind because of the death of her child. She took the dead child in her arms and went from house to house begging people to heal the child. Of course, they could do nothing for her, but finally a follower of Buddha advised her to see him. The Blessed One looked on her with sympathy; and said: 'To heal the child I need some poppy seeds; go and beg four or five poppy seeds from some home where death has never entered.'

So the demented woman went out and sought a house where death had never entered, but in vain. At last, in Buddha's quiet presence, her mind cleared and she understood the meaning of his words. She buried the body, and became one of Buddha's disciples.

(The Teaching of Buddha)

5 Disappointment in God

I was married for twenty years to a wonderful man. He was very encouraging, and loving. He was the worship leader in our church. But two years ago, a very smart pretty girl, aged 21 started coming to our church. She became very friendly with my husband. They were always talking on their own in corners. On Good Friday he said 'Divorce me'. He was starting a new life with this girl. Two weeks after he sent me the divorce papers, she left him and went back to her husband. I prayed so hard that he would do the same. But he was so horrid to me. He would tell me it was my fault, that I was too plain, too small and was nothing. My divorce came through on my twentieth wedding anniversary. I'm so lonely. God has let me down. He said 'I will never leave you or forsake you.' But He has me.

Then I said, 'Lord you understand. Remember me and help me ... You spoke to me, and I listened to every word ... I did not spend my time with other people, laughing and having a good time ... Why do I keep on suffering?

*Why are my wounds incurable? Why won't they heal? Do
you intend to disappoint me like a stream that goes dry in
the summer?' To this the Lord replied: 'If you return, I will
take you back ... If instead of talking nonsense you
proclaim a worthwhile message, you will be my prophet
again.'*

Two complaints about God—the first from a listener in Wales,
desperately hurt by her husband's adultery and blaming God for
it; the other from the Jewish prophet Jeremiah writing 2500 years
ago. God's answer to him was direct enough: 'Stop talking nonsense, and you'll no longer be disappointed.'

'If we believe in God,' said Roy McClelland,

we often have a rather magical vision of who he is, and we
try to bargain; and we hope he will interfere on our side of
our games. It's intriguing that the scapegoats of culture—the
Jewish nation—saw the mythology of it all. The prophets, in
particular, realised that God is not that little god, but the
God who transcends our games.

After the birth of her second son, Sylvia Sands, like many other
women before and since, suffered from postnatal depression.
One of her fellow church-members regarded it as God punishing
her. It was left to someone else to remember God is love:

It was healed for me by a little Chinese woman on the same
ward. She couldn't speak a word of English, and somehow
we reached out together; and I would brush her hair, which
would stop her doing a zoo-walk, pacing up and down, and
when I ran absolutely screaming through the ward, I found
myself held and clasped in her arms. I remember thinking,
'Now this is the real God, in this experience; this is how God
comes to us.' And it's a very feminine image, so my old
image had to go and I became a seeker not a finder.

Sylvia Sands has tried to live that out in her peace work. Yet
what about those who say, 'Hundreds of thousands of people
have prayed millions of prayers for peace, and look where we are
in Bosnia, Rwanda and elsewhere ...'?

I think it depends on your image of God, whether you see
God as superman who swoops down and intervenes; but I

think God sometimes asks you to be feet and hands to your own prayers. True mysticism, I think, is extremely practical.

Jesus certainly never said anywhere, 'Blessed are those who always feel good.' Christians are offered hope; but are not excused from disappointment or depression. Nor was Jesus himself:

When he came in sight of the city, he wept over it and said, 'If only you had known, on this great day, the way that leads to peace! But no; it is hidden from your sight. For a time will come upon you, when your enemies will set up siege-works against you; they will encircle you and hem you in at every point; they will bring you to the ground, you and your children within your walls, and not leave you one stone standing on another, because you did not recognise God's moment when it came.'

Luke 19.41–44 (NEB)

'Tell me the weight of a snowflake,' a coaltit asked a wild dove.

'Nothing more than nothing,' was the answer.

'In that case, I must tell you a marvellous story,' the coaltit said.

'I sat on the branch of a fir, close to its trunk, when it began to snow—not heavily, not in a raging blizzard; no, just like in a dream, without a sound and without any violence. Since I did not have anything better to do, I counted the snowflakes settling on the twigs and needles of my branch. Their number was exactly 3,741,952. When the 3,741,953rd dropped onto the branch—nothing more than nothing, as you say—the branch broke off.'

Having said that, the coaltit flew away.

The dove, since Noah's time, an authority on the matter, thought about the story for a while, and finally said to herself: 'Perhaps there is only one person's voice lacking for peace to come to the world.'

(From New Fables, 'Thus Spoke the Marabou', *Kurt Kauter)*

Meditation

I started on this journey with high hopes. Not that I would
change the world, but that somehow, somewhere I might leave
some sort of mark. Not perhaps a footnote in a history book, but
a recognition by more than just a handful of my fellows that I
had done some good, made a lasting impression. Yet even if the
plaudits weren't too many, then at the end of the journey I, at
least, could look back with satisfaction on what I had achieved.
I started on the journey with high hopes, and now I am more
than half way, I am only too aware those hopes will never be fulfilled, the expectations will be disappointed; for I have not done
half—no, far less than half—of what I might or could have done.
The well of my ideas is dry; I am trapped, trapped by circumstances, limited by cynicism that recognises only the down side
of things and expects the worst of people. Lord, I am disappointed. Disappointed in myself, disappointed in my life, disappointed in you. For despite my feeble groping after faith, I
cannot eliminate the conclusion that you are far away and you
have let me down.

(meditation by the Irish father of a handicapped son)

———

Come God.
Come with the disappointed
Come with the rejected
Come with those who long for something better,
Come and lead us to where you are living
and show us what you want us to do.

****

(Music)

****

Loving Lord,
you fell on your face in a garden.
You know agony from the inside out.

Help us remember there's nowhere
you haven't already been.
At such moments,
let us not be too proud
to fall beside you
and let your agonies begin to soak up ours.

———

So, in trust and faith, we lay open to you the disappointments
that have misshaped our lives,

the hopes that came to nothing,

the injuries we cannot forget and have not forgiven,

Save us from resentment and brooding.

———

Scatter the sin from our souls
as the mist from the hills;
Begin what we do,
Inform what we say,
redeem who we are.

In you we place our hope,
Our great hope, our living hope.

(Iona Community)

Isaiah says:
Listen to me, house of Jacob ...
I have made you and I will bear the burden,
I will carry you and bring you to safety.

Isaiah 46.3–4 (NEB)

* * * * * * * *

(Song)

* * * * * * * *

We believe that your power to heal is still present,
So on your help we call.
We remember others whose hearts are broken because
    love has gone ...
    or because the light they lived by
    has turned to darkness ...
We remember others whose feet walk in circles,
    stopping only when they are tired,
    resting only to walk in circles again ...
We remember others whose flesh and bone or mind and spirit
    are filled with pain ...
We remember others who feel discarded or disposable.

O Christ, put your hands where our prayers beckon.
                                        (Iona Community)

Forgive us
For our false desires
For our self-pity
for all we neglected
or left untended.

****

(Song)

****

St James asks:
*Who is wise and understanding among you? Let him show
it by his good life, by deeds done in the humility that
comes from wisdom. But if you harbour bitter envy and
selfish ambition in your hearts, do not boast about it or
deny the truth. Such 'wisdom' does not come down from
heaven ... For where you have envy and selfish ambition,
there you find disorder and every evil practice. But the
wisdom that comes from heaven is first of all pure; then
peaceloving, considerate, submissive, full of mercy and
good fruit, impartial and sincere.*
                                        James 3.13–18 (NIV)

Lord, make us instruments of your peace;
Where there is hatred, let us sow love;
Where there is injury, pardon;
Where there is doubt, faith;
Where there is despair, hope;
Where there is darkness, light;
Where there is sadness, joy.
O divine master, grant that I may not so much seek
To be consoled, as to console,
To be understood, as to understand,
To be loved, as to love,
For it is in giving that we receive;
It is in pardoning that we are pardoned;
It is in dying that we are born to eternal life.

(St Francis, thirteenth century)

We dedicate our homes to you and your work as the God of Peace.
May they be a place of joy, laughter, and freedom,
A place of rest for those who are weary,
A place of hope for those who have become disillusioned,
A place of healing and comfort for those who are broken and hurt,
A place of forgiveness for those who seek a new way of life,
A place of encouragement for those who hunger and thirst for peace and justice,
A place of vision and inspiration for all those who seek a new and better way for our country.

Dear God, who made Wisdom before all else,
Who chose her as his darling and delight,
Fill us too with wisdom and understanding,
that we, like her, may not be disappointed,
but play in your presence for ever. Amen.

****

(Music)

****

Some Suggestions for Worship Music

1 'A Gentle Place' from *Banba*, by Clannad (BMG/RCA).
2 'Sancta Brigida' sung by Noirin Ni Riain, from LP *Caoineadh Maighdine* (Gael Linn).
3 'Sarabande' by Bach, from *Cello Suite*.
4 'Sarabande' by Grieg, from *Holberg Suite*.

Other Music

5 Song: 'Yesterday' by Lennon and McCartney, from CD *The Beatles*, 1962-66 (EMI/Apple).
6 Song: 'Mother' by John Lennon, from LP *Barbra Joan Streisand* (Northern Songs Ltd/CBS).
7 'Na Laethe Bhl' ('Yesterday is Gone') by Clannad (BMG/RCA).

****

DR ANNE TOWNSEND *was a missionary doctor in Thailand for sixteen years. Back in England, she became founding editor of* Christian Family *magazine and then director of CARE Trust. The story of her subsequent emotional crisis and recovery is shared in one of her books,* Faith without Pretending. *It describes her journey from a strict evangelical form of Christianity, and her discovery of a theology that she believes has now brought her closer to God.*

As a result of this radical reassessment of her life, she trained as an Anglican priest and a counsellor, became a chaplain with a major London hospital, and worked with cancer patients for four years.

A grandmother and mother of three, and dean for ministers in secular employment in the Southwark diocese, she is among the first wave of women to be ordained priest in the Church of England in 1994. Now her vocation as a priest is expressed in her full-time work as a professional counsellor. She is also training in Jungian analysis.

Born in Manchester, MIKE WILSON *was an insurance broker, investment adviser and co-partner in a family business with his father, D. C. Wilson and Partners. This firm went into liquidation in 1988, following the collapse of the financial company, Barlow Clowes. He is now a freelance business writer, a financial adviser, and director of an evangelistic organisation, the Seamen's Christian Friend Society. He is also involved in Covenanters, a back-up service for churches who want to improve their youth work.*

Today he and his wife, ROS WILSON, *live with their two children in Bramhall. Both are members of 'Open Brethren', an independent evangelical church, which is an offshoot of the Plymouth Brethren. Ros is a part-time health visitor.*

FIVE

Stress

*Everyone became alarmed when they saw Mulla
Nasruddin mounted on his ass, charging through the
streets of the village.*
'Where are you off to, Mullah?' they asked.
*'I'm searching for my ass,' said the Mullah as he
whizzed by.*

———

Mullah Nasruddin, charging through an Islamic legend about the
follies and delights of human nature—a more picturesque version of looking for spectacles, which all along are planted firmly on the nose. To begin with, it is comic; but if Nasruddin goes
on and on, whizzing round in ever-diminishing circles, the
stress and its consequences can be devastating.

Passion Sunday recalls the stress of Christ's betrayal, torture,
mockery, abandonment, and hideous death. Unlike the stress of
Nasruddin (who may even enjoy his self-induced anxiety), this
is no mere foolishness, but hard agony that had to be endured.

So when is stress inevitable, and when is it self-created? How
can we avoid unnecessary stress? What has helped people
through it? Letters from listeners covered financial stress, stress
over relationships at home and at work; stress about what others
thought; the stress of carers; and much more.

———

**I had been doing too much. A feeling of strain began to
develop, because of my old weakness, wanting to excel at**

everything and trying to help more people than I have the
emotional or spiritual resources for.

(London)

[Five years ago, my husband died of cancer.] At the same time,
a Dutch firm went into liquidation in our dried flower business
owing us a lot of money. [So after nursing my husband 24
hours a day, and at the same time running the business, with
two children at boarding school] I was left with all these debts
and him dying. Then I nursed my father, who died this last
year of cancer as well. My brother and sister have not given
me any help or support. One of my children is about to start a
course which I've got to find money for, and I just can't go on
... I've coped with the grief, I've coped with the loss, I've been
coping up to now, with the stress, but I'm just about at the
end of my tether.

(Devon)

I was head of a department; I was therefore under pressure to
perform, to produce fees. I had to look after the well-being of
my team—all the things that business people come up against.
For three years, I was getting more and more stressed.

(London)

My son was killed, I lost my job, my ex-wife deserted me, and
my mother was stricken with Alzheimer's Disease. You think,
my God, this is like a soap-opera, but it really is true.
Anyway, I've coped, I'm surviving.

(West Sussex)

———

Mike Wilson is a former investment broker. In 1988, just after he
had moved into a new house, with a larger mortgage, his business went into liquidation. The failure of the business (which he
reckons could once have been sold for perhaps a million
pounds) was caused by the collapse of Barlow Clowes and
Partners, with whom his clients had invested fifteen million
pounds:

We lost track of the numbers of writs that were served on us. There was a lot of litigation, and a lot of angry people. Over and above that, we were interviewed by the serious fraud office. We even had some people sitting in my own lounge, asking me some very, very difficult questions. It made me feel a bit like a criminal; but fortunately it all got resolved quite happily.

To begin with, the most immediate effect on Ros Wilson, Mike's wife, was confusion: 'I was just very, very fearful. I didn't understand a lot of the legalities, and I just literally had to live from day to day and see how the story unfolded.'

Ten years ago, Dr Anne Townsend was an apparently successful former magazine editor, a trained doctor, and a director of a charity, in much demand as a lecturer and writer. Yet she tried to commit suicide:

I'd had enormous expectations of myself, and so had everybody else of me; and I was desperately living up to what I was supposed to be being. My husband was abroad a lot with his work with TEAR Fund, a third world charity; and we had a relative with a very chronic severe illness that was totally disrupting our family life. I was finding it increasingly impossible to hold down a job, where (very stupidly) I was leaving at five o'clock in the morning to go to work, getting back fairly late in the evening, working all hours, plus [coping with] this ill relative, and two sons, doing GCSE and A levels. Plus it began to feel that God had really let me down. That was the worst of all.

Like Mike and Ros, in the past Anne had faced financial problems too (though of a different kind), as had a number of listeners. They ranged from owners of substantial country houses, to those on the dole on council estates, and a Sri Lankan refugee in France.

1 Financial Stress

Nine years ago, my husband left me with two boys aged eleven and twelve. He never cared. He never even sent them a Christmas card, or a penny, or anything. All I could do was look for part-time jobs, so that I could keep the house going. And we had debts.

I am a widow of 71, no children. In 1978, my accountant
suggested I join Lloyds. They now say I owe them £370,000—
considerably more than I own. I have in the last two years
moved to a smaller house, and moved my 85-year-old sister
out of her cottage into a home. I walked about for some weeks
in a daze, feeling like an empty tight-stringed violin. Nowadays
I *dread* the post, as I *dread* losing this semi-detached house.

(Wiltshire)

I owe Lloyds about £300,000. After my husband's death, my
son was badly bullied at school and last year, I received a
telephone call from my son's public school saying he was
threatening to commit suicide and throw himself off the roof.
Lying awake at night alone in a house isolated on a Scottish
hillside, I have reached depths of despair I would rather not
think about.

———

Mike Wilson never hit the depths of despair, but his financial
problems hardly made for calm:

At one level, the stress wasn't too bad, because the roller
coaster of the problem itself, and having to deal with it, kept
me going. I was kept very, very busy, and to a small extent I
felt I was able to do something about the situation. Having
said that, yes, obviously I did suffer from stress. The typical
symptoms were a funny taste in the mouth, sometimes for-
getting what I was supposed to be doing, or what I was supposed to be saying. I can look back and see that I was
stressed, but I think I found it a lot easier than Ros did.

Ros Wilson agreed that, on the surface, that is how it would
appear:

I felt that Mike, being on the front line, was actually getting
information first hand; and he seemed to be coping with all
of it, he was doing something. I was just sat at home waiting
for news. And I began to think that maybe this won't be too
bad; but then I would watch the television news reports or I
would read a newspaper, and I would think, 'Goodness, this

is terrible, I should be worried,' and so I'd find myself running round in the day, trying to find something to fill my time positively, and yet achieving nothing.

For eleven months, they had no income. Another listener knew that experience well; when the recession put paid to his business, he was forced on to the dole:

This meant a drastic drop in income. Over the last year or so, this has entailed debts mounting up to perhaps £5,000. As a consequence of the drop in income, this has meant that we've just not been able to afford things you normally take for granted, like clothing, general repairs to the home, and specifically my car. I'm not for one minute going to say 'I don't worry.' Of course I worry, but I try very hard to keep hold of these promises that the Bible teaches:

I tell you, do not worry about your life, what you will eat or drink; or about your body, what you will wear. Is not life more important than food, and the body more important than clothes? Look at the birds of the air; they do not sow or reap or store away in barns, and yet your heavenly Father feeds them. Are you not much more valuable than they? Who of you by worrying can add a single hour to his life?

And why do you worry about clothes? See how the lilies of the field grow. They do not labour or spin. Yet I tell you that not even Solomon in all his splendour was dressed like one of these. If that is how God clothes the grass of the field, which is here today and tomorrow is thrown into the fire, will he not much more clothe you, O you of little faith? So do not worry, saying, 'What shall we eat?' or 'What shall we drink?' or 'What shall we wear?' For the pagans run after all these things, and your heavenly Father knows that you need them. But seek first his kingdom and his righteousness, and all these things will be given to you as well. Therefore do not worry about tomorrow, for tomorrow will worry about itself. Each day has enough trouble of its own.

Matthew 6.25–34 (NIV)

Ros Wilson too tried to keep hold of those promises:

> They are beautiful, reassuring words, but at the time, they really didn't mean anything to me, because I was praying and praying, and things just kept getting worse. And how do you not worry? We had a young family, and the effect of Barlow Clowes had spread so far, by that time I'd really stopped worrying about the birds of the air, it was me on the ground I was more worried about! So I found it difficult at that time to apply those words.

In the end, her anxiety turned out to be unnecessary. Ros and Mike did not have to sell their home; Ros returned to work:

> I didn't feel it was right to stay at home and pray 'Lord, provide,' when in fact he had. I had qualifications that would get me a job that would earn enough to pay the mortgage. So that was the decision I made, and applied for a job and went back to work.

For some years, Anne Townsend had worked as a doctor in Thailand. I wondered if, at that time, she might have been delighted to have Ros and Mike's standard of living, even *after* the collapse of their business?

> Yes, the missionary society I was working with didn't give us any fixed income; so we really had very little indeed. I remember one occasion when there just wasn't very much money, and I had to choose between buying a tube of toothpaste or buying stamps to post a letter home. And I really found those words about God providing what I needed very hard to grab hold of. It sometimes seemed as if he didn't; other times it seemed as if God did provide.

To the local Thai villagers, Ros and Mike would have seemed unbelievably wealthy:

> Their standards seemed to be different from ours. There was a Buddhist saying: 'There are always rice in the fields, and fish in the river.' And there are. People lived very simply round where we were, in little wooden houses up on stilts, with very little furniture. Most people had a television set, and that was what mattered; but there was enough to eat, and people weren't starving. Things were simpler, a

different way of looking at life. Things they kept as precious were things we would throw away, like empty cotton reels, and Coca Cola cans. Things were made from them.

Socrates believed that the wise person would instinctively lead a frugal life, and he himself would not even wear shoes. Yet he delighted in the market-place, and often went there to look at the wares on display. When asked why, he said he loved discovering how many things he was perfectly happy without.

But today in the West, our expectations are different. The listeners from Wiltshire and Scotland (quoted above) described what helped them through their financial difficulties:

> **How have I coped?** God, gin, arnica (homoeopathic treatment for shock), a Jewish lawyer who is constantly supportive and understanding, a beloved niece and a host of friends who surround me with care. Every morning I ask God's help through the day. He shows me many people who need my help and who in fact in their turn help me—two 90-year-olds, cancer cases, others financially distressed. God has also left me my health.
>
> **(Wiltshire)**

> **My mother has been the source of huge support and strength, and I can feel a response to prayer when she, my sister and I pray together. But you can perhaps understand why I often feel like Job in the Bible, and I pray very hard that I have his faith.**

In all his misfortunes, Job was unlucky with his friends: they kept on telling him it was all his fault. One particular friend of Ros Wilson definitely did not do that:

> She telephoned me almost as soon as the news had broken about Barlow Clowes, and when the allegations to the intermediaries had been made. She just said, 'Look, I don't care if you've done anything, whatever the situation is, I don't care, I'm here if you need me.' As indeed lots of my friends did. They just rallied round in a way that, sometimes I'm ashamed to say, in the days now it's easier, I forget.

2 Stress about What Others Think

The Master seemed quite impervious to what people thought of him. When the disciples asked how he had attained this stage of inner freedom, he laughed aloud and said: 'Till I was twenty I did not care what people thought of me. After twenty, I worried endlessly about what my neighbours thought. Then one day after fifty, I suddenly saw that they hardly ever thought of me at all.

────────

I went through a period of anxiety and fear caused primarily through the physical exhaustion of having children and living so publicly as a [church] minister's wife. Everything was noted. Where I was, who came for dinner, who I spoke to, how I spent my leisure time. Was I interested in the bazaars, the fund-raising, ad nauseam. It was followed by very low esteem, and a fall-out of self confidence. My salvation was returning to work (as a teacher) and beginning to be a separate person again. I used to pray for strength for the next fifteen minutes or one hour. As I came through those periods, the time lengthened ... I wrote to God and 'showed' them to him, then put them on the fire.

(Gwent)

To Anne Townsend, too, the anxiety of what other people thought, and the fear she might lose their support and approval, was a real pressure:

That was the most terrifying thing for me, because I think all my life I have lived to please other people, up to the last few years when I've discovered I don't have to. Ever since I was a little girl I've been doing it. So the fear of losing other people's approval was terrifying. And that made it very difficult for me to say to other people, 'I can't do this by myself, will somebody help me?' I found it impossible to say that. I had to make a dramatic gesture.

That dramatic gesture was attempted suicide. One of the extra pressures on Anne Townsend was that on top of the family problems she described earlier, she had also been going round the country, speaking on various platforms about the importance of a strong, stable family:

> That was a kind of nightmare, because there I was trying to pretend to be Mrs Perfect-Wife-and-Mother, and things were crumbling around me at home. It was the hypocrisy of it all. It was a way of coping—I'm thinking of the cope that a priest wears that covers everything up. I was covering up what was going on inside me by all these activities up on platforms. Very hard to know which was the real me.

The stress at work was in a way, she says, self-made:

> It was a small new organisation, and I was having to work really hard to deliver the goods, because once the goods were delivered, people would send in money to support us. So I was getting the 5.15 morning train into work—a completely ludicrous idea—as well as coping with very demanding phone calls from people with horrendous needs and insoluble problems without the back-up support I needed to be dealing with that sort of thing.

And then she would go home, and get the tea:

> And there would be my sick relative, and whatever might have been happening at home, plus I was writing a lot then, and I would sit down and write. It was a chaotic, crazy existence. I had got into a kind of cycle where I was blotting out what was going on inside me, and the increasing stress, by doing more work; so I didn't have to think about it. To sleep at night, there were sleeping pills and a glass of wine.

3 Stress at Home and at Work

The poet Roger McGough was with his first wife for ten years, and was reluctant to get a divorce for various reasons, including the children, even though the marriage was in difficulties. In a book called *Stress Survivors*, chronicling the experiences of a number of people, he described to the author the stress of being in a relationship when he wanted to be somewhere else. But he and his wife carried on and on, and that, he said, was the worst part. Eventually they did separate, culminating in divorce over a period of five years. It was a very stressful, awkward and difficult time, coping with day-to-day things. He was working very hard, his mother was dying, and the children were taken from him. He reckons his stress probably showed in heavy drinking. He also used to spend a lot of time in bed.

Another listener described other forms of stress. In his forties, a vet with a wife and two girls, he lives in a nice home, and enjoys his job. He has good health mostly, except when stress steals it. Up to about the age of 35, stress switched itself on and off according to pressure of work, and the fear of doing something at work for the first time. After 35, the pressures of responsibility mounted—young children, restoring a derelict home, money swallowed up in purchasing a partnership, a practice needing to be built up. In his case, symptoms of stress are a painful face, sore eyes, inability to think properly, working on autopilot, and uncoordinated limbs:

> Stress creeps up on you when you're not expecting it, and because there's no single cause, you're paralysed to do anything about it.
>
> Emotions: Frustration. Wasted days—joy stolen. 'Surely goodness and mercy will follow me all the days of my life'— that's what should be left in my wake. But stress makes simple jobs look difficult, go wrong, and blocks a happy rapport between farmer and vet. Joy puts you in control, gives you authority.
>
> 'Lord Jesus, please heal me.'
>
> Answer—'You're perfectly healthy, but look at the agenda you set yourself. How about being less hyperactive—thinking ahead more, and channelling your energies more?'

He says things are now improving rapidly; maybe he is following the answer to his prayer.

Yet many people refuse to take even the first step of acknowledging their stress—like, for some years, this chartered surveyor:

> I used to wake up at two o'clock, couldn't get back to sleep, I used to wake up at three o'clock, couldn't get back to sleep, I

used to get up at five o'clock, start work, and then at seven
o'clock go and wake up the rest of the family. And a lot of that
time, I was not acknowledging the fact. So when my wife said I
am coming to the doctor with you, I thought, 'Something must
be up.' And when she explained all these symptoms to the
doctor, that was when I acknowledged that I was suffering
from stress and that I was depressed. In the end I think I was
off for about five weeks.

---

*'How would spirituality help a man of the world like me?',
said the businessman.
    'It will help you to have more,' said the Master.
    'How?'
    'By teaching you to desire less.'*

Anne Townsend's problem was complicated in that she thought
what she desired was what the Lord desired:

> I felt I was a candle that had to be burnt at both ends for God;
> and inevitably I shrunk very quickly. I felt I had to be doing
> things for God the whole time, and it wasn't until after my
> suicide attempt that I suddenly began to realise that it was
> *who* I was that mattered to God—not what I was doing, but
> the kind of person I was being. I hadn't really thought about
> that very much before, other than being the kind of person
> who did a lot of things.

I commented that Jesus enjoyed himself at weddings, had a glass
of wine, teased his friends, cooked fish at the side of the Sea of
Galilee ...

> Absolutely, and it was quite new for me to begin to enjoy
> doing little things as well as big things. I worked for a while
> in a department store in the fashion department, touching
> satin and velvet, and feeling fabrics. Very different. I hadn't
> had time to do any of this sort of thing before.

Perhaps the one huge difference between the stress of most of us, and the stress of Christ as described in the Gospels, is that his stress was caused by the agony of facing reality, not evading it. When Anne Townsend was most stressed, the Passion story, she said, did not have much to say to her:

It seemed that God was right outside, nothing to do with what was going on for me. Then I began to realise that God was actually there in the mess and the horribleness and the awfulness of it all—that Jesus was part of it, because he'd been through it himself at the end of his life. It was amazing for me to find that.

Jesus then came with his disciples to a place called Gethsemane. He said to them, 'Sit here while I go over there to pray.' He took with him Peter and the two sons of Zebedee. Anguish and dismay came over him, and he said to them, 'My heart is ready to break with grief. Stop here, and stay awake with me.' He went on a little, fell on his face in prayer, and said, 'My Father, if it is possible, let this cup pass me by. Yet not as I will, but as thou wilt.'

He came to the disciples and found them asleep; and he said to Peter, 'What! Could none of you stay awake with me one hour? Stay awake, and pray that you may be spared the test. The spirit is willing, but the flesh is weak.

Matthew 26.36–41 (NEB)

4 Relieving Stress

Ros Wilson says the support of her work colleagues after the collapse of Mike's business was superb; yet for some time the effects of stress were very much to the fore. There was a strange taste in her mouth; she had problems sleeping; she was tired all the time, and a bit breathless:

At that point, I decided I was anaemic, and took myself off to my doctor, and said, 'Could I please have some iron?' He took my pulse, and he smiled and he put down his pen, and he said, 'So what else is going on in your life, Ros?' And at that point, I just burst into tears. I was just mortified that I cried in the doctor's surgery. You just didn't do that. I really felt I'd let myself down, but I think that was the beginning of my really facing the fact that I was stressed.

He told her to go home, and to take twenty minutes out of every day, and find a place where nobody could get to her:

And that was the bathroom. And he said, 'Regardless of whether you fill the bath or not, lock yourself in there for twenty minutes, and put a notice on the door which says, "I am in here, and I intend to stay in here for twenty minutes, and the first one who shouts 'Mum' gets their legs broken!" ' So the children understood that this was my time out, that I needed this time to recoup.

Anne Townsend did not lock herself into the bathroom, but she did manage to get herself out of her job. After her suicide attempt, she couldn't carry on with it any more:

That meant we hadn't got a second income, so we couldn't pay the mortgage. So we had to be quite dramatic about this, and sell our house, and, that way, pay off the mortgage. That way, we were able to buy a very small flat, so I didn't have to be working full-time, and had space for myself.

Soon she was being kinder to herself, no longer forcing herself to do all those things. Sex became something to rediscover and enjoy, and there were other pleasures too:

I remember the great luxury of walking round Woolworths and buying fifty pence worth of selected sweets, and just enjoying them for me; and then beginning to go out for walks, and find time to enjoy things that I hadn't done for years and years and years.

———

The industrialist was horrified to find the Indonesian fisherman lying beside his boat, smoking a pipe.
'Why aren't you out fishing?' said the industrialist.
'Because I have caught enough fish for the day.'
'Why don't you catch some more?'
'What would I do with it?'
'Earn more money. Then you could have a motor fixed to your boat and go into deeper waters and catch more fish. That would bring you more money to buy nylon nets, so more fish, more money. Soon you would have enough to

buy two boats ... even a fleet of boats. Then you could be
rich like me. Then you could really enjoy life.'
   The fisherman looked at him, with a slow smile: 'What
do you think I am doing now?'
                                    (Song of the Bird, *Anthony de Mello*)

5 Stress of Carers

I am 48 years old, live alone, and am deputy head of a large
rural comprehensive school. Since last October, I have been
off work due to anxiety. As with so many anxiety states, there
is no single cause, but rather a combination of factors. These
include:

pressures at work, exacerbated by last-minute changes in the
national curriculum;

attempting to resolve a five-year subsidence problem at home,
dealing with unhelpful insurers, then having workmen
dismantling my home and reassembling it over a period of six
months;

worry and guilt over my 91-year-old highly confused mother,
who lives in a local residential home;

concern over my nephew who has muscular dystrophy;

relationships;

the desire to strengthen the links which I established between
our local community and one in Albania—but involving
problems raising money, organising transport and
communicating;

and anger that so many thing seem to have piled up at once!

That story reflected something that emerged again and again in
letters: that people often deal with short-term pressure very well
(and even thrive on the challenge and excitement); but that long-
term stress, particularly when a whole series of stressful circumstances combine, is another kettle of sea monsters altogether—
and one that often needs a quite different approach.

One of the hardest things for carers to cope with is long-term mental decline or madness in the person they are caring for, like the man in the Bible who called himself Legion. One listener from the Chelmsford area cared for years for her schizophrenic mother:

> 'I was there', trying to understand a poor soul who, like the man in the Gospel, could well say, 'My name is Legion, for we are many.' I had to grow to understand that in all the bizarre behaviour and selfishness, it was the disease speaking and not the person—though there were times when I could cheerfully have done her mischief. I think about all those others whose names are Legion, and for those who care for them, especially at home, with very little to guide them, and often at their wits' end. I had a lifetime to learn. For those to whom it happens in mid- and late life, it can be devastating.
>
> But through it all, I learned the eternal God is thy refuge and underneath are the everlasting arms. None of our family ever fell out of those arms.

Another listener's husband died after ten years of what was thought to be Alzheimer's disease, a form of dementia in which the sufferer's short-term memory disintegrates:

> I went through anger, disbelief, and finally acceptance, not so much of the disease, but of my inability to cope. It was in the last months of his life that I said to the Lord, 'I admit I can't cope any longer. I am giving this burden to you. Please help me.' After that, things began to happen. People helped me more and because I allowed people to see my vulnerability, I was amazed how doors opened.
>
> Of course, it had been my fault, never allowing people to see me not coping. Pride is a very bad thing. I have learnt a lot by this experience, specially about myself.

As a health visitor, Ros Wilson sees many people at their wits' end trying to deal with elderly or ill or mentally ill relatives. She says she is usually called in as almost a last resort.

You really need to talk to people about giving themselves permission not to cope. Because when you are caring for a member of your family, as Anne was, it's very difficult to view it as being something to share. It's very hard to say to somebody, 'I can't carry this burden', because you feel the responsibility is yours to carry. You feel we've got to see this through. And I think it's hard for them to relinquish that.

Yet sometimes, if they do not get help, they cannot carry on for long. Anne Townsend's mother, now in her mid-eighties, nursed Anne's father for more than a year before he died. She did come to realise she needed help, and not only got it from outside, but realised she needed to help herself too:

Suddenly she realised there were two of them - and that she had to look after herself as well as him. That meant giving herself permission to watch her favourite television programme every day. That made such a difference.

Or even perhaps having a day off or a holiday even?

Well, she never had a day off or a holiday, but it did mean going on the local bus into town for two and a half hours and letting the cleaning lady be at home with my father. It made such a difference once she let herself do that.

6   Stress of Illness

I cried every day for all of the twelve weeks of treatment—not from self-pity, but just from the stress of coping—crying was my unconscious safety and pressure valve.

Just before my chemotherapy began, members from my Baptist church came to our sitting room, and very quietly and in an attitude of caring and sharing, did just what it says in James, chapter 5. They prayed over me and anointed me with oil. I found it hard to confess my sins of criticism and selfishness in their presence. But I felt it was right to follow what the Bible says. I came to realise that I could help myself. I began to share my feelings more openly with a few friends from church. I began to try and keep a diary.

Although I had often read my Bible, I decided to begin to read through the Bible, book by book. The seriousness of my situation made me read it as if I had never read it before— eager to know what Jesus said and did when he was on earth. Eager for God to speak to me through the Bible each day. I found enormous help. Gradually, I felt a deeper and a closer relationship with God.

I felt and knew that God loved me personally. He was helping and encouraging me in so many ways—a rota of friends to take me to and from the weekly treatments; sympathetic staff and doctors at the hospital; three delicious meals brought weekly by different people from the church; a lovely wig. My friends continued to pray for me. I experienced peace in my heart.

On November 7th, I suddenly realised I was thankful that I had had this experience of cancer, and bone marrow transplant. With that realisation came a lifting of the stress and pressure.

(Glasgow, woman)

Anne Townsend worked for a while as a chaplain in one of the major London hospitals. She thought at first that patients would like it if she went round and cheered them up. It failed. She then tried something different. That was simply sitting with people in the mess, just being with them in all the horribleness:

There was one lady, who had a horrible cancer that made her corner of the ward smell to high heaven. She said to me it was if as she had a septic tank running through her body, and she hated this. I learned just to go and sit and be with her day after day after day in the awfulness, remembering that Jesus was there sitting in it with us. I didn't say very much to her about it. Somehow the fact that I was there with her, as God's representative in all that, transformed and changed things. It did something in her I found very hard to understand. After a few months, she entered the church and was a Christian before she died.

*One day the Chao Chou fell down in the snow and cried
out, 'Help me up, help me up!' A monk ran over and lay
beside him. Chao Chou got up and walked away.*
(Zen Buddhist story)

Meditation

Lord, I get so busy.
Sometimes because I want to help.
Sometimes because I can't say no.
Sometimes because I'm flattered to be asked.
And it all adds up to strain, to tiredness,
to not having two minutes to call my own.
And then comes the bad temper, the resentment.
And before long, I'm hating the people who asked me.
Hating the people who want my help.
And then I feel guilty, and then I hate them more.

Lord, I feel like a mouse in a treadmill.
Rushing around faster and faster,
Getting nowhere.
And the first thing that goes out of the window is you.
No time, Lord, sorry!
Then my family.
They should know I'm busy and not ask for my time.
And my friends.
Can't they see all the things I have to do?

... Lord, still my heart.
Help me cut down on the adrenalin.
Give me your peace.
(From A Silence and a Shouting)

* * * * * * * *

(Music)

* * * * * * * *

O God, before whose face
we are not made righteous
even by being right:
free us from the need
to justify ourselves
by our own anxious striving,

that we may be abandoned
to faith in you alone. Amen.

(Janet Morley)

Dear God, you hold in the palm of your hand all whose stress is
overwhelming, who cannot see you;

who are anxious or fearful, exhausted or ill,
who feel we cannot go on.

You wait grieving alongside all whose lives are choked with
overwork or consumption;
who are afraid of failing;
who, even when we achieve our ambitions, never feel satisfied.

And, like a parent whose child is learning to walk, you watch all
who have begun to find you, but are overwhelmed;
those for whom the risk of healing is too painful;
who are afraid of your embrace,
and fear your energetic power
to transform our lives.

Lord, these whom you love, are suffering.
Set us free to hear your voice.

———

God of the weary
receive our tiredness
God of the hungry
know our emptiness
God of those in danger
hold our fear
God of the silenced
hear our despair
God of the heavyladen
give us rest
God of the hopeful
fill us again with longing.

(Janet Morley)

Jesus said: 'Come to me, all whose work is hard, whose load is heavy; and I will give you relief.'
                                    Matthew 11.28 (NEB)

* * * * * * * * *

(Song)

* * * * * * * * *

*Light of light, you have searched me out and known me.
You know where I am and where I go,
You see my thoughts from afar.
You discern my paths and my resting places,
You are acquainted with all my ways.
Yes, and not a word comes from my lips
but you, O God, have heard it already.
You are in front of me and behind me,
you have laid your hand on my shoulder.
Such knowledge is too wonderful for me,
So great that I cannot fathom it.*

*Where shall I go from your Spirit,
where shall I flee from your Presence?
If I climb to the heavens you are there:
if I descend to the depths of the earth, you are there also.
If I spread my wings towards the morning,
And fly to the uttermost shores of the sea,
Even there your hand will lead me,
and your right hand will hold me.
If I should cry to the darkness to cover me,
and the night to enclose me,
the darkness is no darkness to you,
and the night is as clear as the day ...
... How deep are your thoughts to me, O God,
How great is the sum of them.
Were I to count them they are more in number
than the grains of sand upon the sea shore—
and still I would know nothing about you—
yet still would you hold me in the palm of your hand.*
                    (from Psalm 139, Jim Cotter's version)

Mother Julian says:
This is the cause why we are not at rest in heart and soul:
that here we seek rest in things that are so small, there is
no rest in them, and we do not know our God who is all
mighty, all wise and all good. For he is true rest. ...

For he is endless and has made us for his own self only,
and has restored us by his blessed Passion, and keeps us
in his blessed love. And he does all this through his
goodness.

God of your goodness, give me yourself, for you are
enough for me.
                (*from* Revelations of Divine Love, *fourteenth century*)

****

(Music)

****

Loving Lord, who needs not our work, but our love,
Help us to live in the here and now, to do the next thing we have
to do with our whole heart, and to find delight in doing it.
(prayer based on Meister Eckhart, fourteenth century)

Keep on loving each other as sisters and brothers. Do not
forget to entertain strangers, for by so doing some people
have entertained angels without knowing it.

Remember those in prison as if you were their fellow
prisoners, and those who are ill-treated as if you
yourselves were suffering.

Marriage should be honoured by all, and the marriage
bed kept pure; for God will judge the adulterer and all the
sexually immoral.

Keep your lives free from the love of money and be
content with what you have, because God has said,
'Never will I leave you, never will I forsake you.'
So we say with confidence, 'The Lord is my helper,
I will not be afraid.'
                            Hebrews 13.1–6 (NIV)

O Christ, the Master Carpenter
Who, at the last, through wood and nails,
Purchased our whole salvation.
Wield well your tools in the workshop of your world,
So that we, who come rough-hewn to your bench,
May here be fashioned to a truer beauty of your hand. Amen.

(Iona Community)

And may the God whose first word is 'peace be with you'
Help us make peace with ourselves.

May God bless us in our sleep with rest,
In our dreams with vision,
In our waking with a calm mind,
In our souls with the friendship of the Holy Spirit
This day and always. Amen.

(Iona Community)

(Music)

****

Some Suggestions for Worship Music

1 'The Orient' by Dick Walter, from CD *The Editor's Companion 5* (KPM Music).
2 'Cosmos' by Shaw/Rogers, from LP *Space* (Carlin).
3 *Concerto for Clarinet* by Aaron Copland.
4 'Loving Shepherd of Thy Sheep' by John Rutter, from CD *Hail, Gladdening Light* (OUP/Collegium Records).
5 'Be Thou My Vision' by John Rutter, from LP *Te Deum* (OUP/Collegium Records).

Other Music

6 'Nervous Breakdown' by Carleen Anderson, from CD *Nervous Breakdown* (MCA Music/Circa Records).
7 *Partita no. 2* by J. S. Bach.
8 *Oboe Concerto* by Richard Strauss.
9 'Lean on Me' by Bill Withers, from LP *Women in (E)Motion* (Interior Music Inc/GEMA).

SEAN WILLIAMS *is the sales director of a small company in the oil industry. He went to school in Wiltshire, and spent much of his twenties climbing rocks and mountains. After teaching for a while, he worked for Shell in the oil industry in Manchester, selling lubricants, then petrol. After a few years in London in marketing, he came back to Manchester as a UK sales manager, before beginning his present job. He has three children, one by his first marriage, two by his second.*

KATHLEEN RICHARDSON *lives and works in West Yorkshire. A Methodist minister, she is currently the Moderator of the Free Church Federal Council, and a past President of the Methodist Conference (the first woman to hold that post). She has a disabled husband, and three grown-up daughters.*

SIX

Guilt

An ancient rabbi once asked his pupils how they could tell
when the night had ended and the day was on its way
back.

'Could it be', asked one student, 'when you can see an
animal in the distance and tell whether it is a sheep or a
dog?'

'No,' answered the rabbi.

'Could it be', asked another, 'when you can look at a
tree in the distance and tell whether it is a fig tree or a
peach tree?'

'No,' said the rabbi.

'Well, then, what is it?' his pupils demanded.

'It is when you look on the face of any woman or man
and see that she or he is your sister or brother. Because if
you cannot do this, then, no matter what time it is, it is
still night.'

Guilt is like that disturbing first moment of dawn in that old
Jewish story, when we realise that people we have abandoned, or
insulted, or denied, or betrayed in the dark, were all along our
brothers and sisters. It is the moment of revelation, when we
know we should have acted differently; when we realise that
things we may once have persuaded ourselves were done for the
benefit of others, were really done for the benefit of ourselves.

It should be, and sometimes is, not only the gateway to mourning, but to morning, to forgiveness, reconciliation, and a change
for the better. Yet if unresolved, it casts its poisonous twilight for
years. For Judas, the betrayer of Christ, the dawn of realising

what he had done was so dreary that he hanged himself. Others are stunned by the advancing light; they feel unworthy of it, and retreat into another night—hating themselves. Others already rarely feel anything but unworthy, conned into believing they deserve the burdens they and others have placed on their backs.

Letters and calls came from people who in some cases had for years carried round unresolved feelings of guilt:

Nineteen years ago, my husband died suddenly from a heart attack. About five years later, I had a tremendous attack of guilt that I hadn't called the doctor more quickly. I felt I was responsible for his death.

(Wirral)

My widowed mother died suddenly, after being housebound for five years. During her last pain-racked years, I would quite often treat her in a needlessly harsh or thoughtless manner. I feel ashamed at the ingratitude I showed her for the many sacrifices she made on my behalf.

(London)

Due to a combination of circumstances, my husband took his own life. Later I attempted to take my life. I longed for someone to say 'it could not have been your fault', but no one did. After all these years, I am still lacerated by these memories, and in my bad moments, blame myself for all that has happened.

(Cheshire)

I am 78. Loneliness, guilt, fear, stress, complete helplessness, that's me. There's nothing much I can say about it, except a lot of it is my own fault. I have complete and utter self-disgust and hopelessness. That's it.

(Newcastle-upon-Tyne)

Kathleen Richardson has been through the guilt of divided loyalties—a desperately ill husband at home, and a job as a national Free Church leader that took up more and more time.

Increasingly, she was not sure what to do for the best: 'I felt I was expected to cope with it all, and it was all my fault that I seemed to be failing so dismally in just about everything.'

That was not other people's perception of it, but her own. Because of a brain tumour, her husband has been unable to work for ten years and has had repeated operations.

Last summer, he became so ill that they attempted a very aggressive surgery and didn't hold out very much hope at all, and I prayed for him to die. I thought at the time that seemed to be the only way out of a situation that seemed to be becoming unbearable. Afterwards he lived, and I had to face the guilt of feeling that I'd wanted to take things into my own hands. He now says he is glad to be alive, and I am beginning to be glad with him too.

Sean Williams is a marketing man in the oil industry, formerly an alcoholic. Alcoholism is increasingly regarded these days as an illness, in which alcoholics drink from compulsion and not from free choice. Yet he, like others, is now off the booze. He remembers clearly the moment of choice:

I'd been to a dinner in London, and before that dinner I'd made a promise to myself that, OK, I was going to drink (because I had to be sociable), but I wasn't going to get drunk and end up in the mess I usually did in these circumstances. I can remember the moment—it was about 10.30 at night— when somebody said to me, 'What's the matter with you? Come on, why don't you have a proper drink?' And handed me a large Scotch. And I said, 'Yeah, what's wrong with me?' I lost control and got horrendously drunk yet again.

He woke up the following morning full of guilt and remorse, and the knowledge that yet again he had failed:

I remember driving up the motorway—I was on the M6—in floods of tears, completely out of control. I just shouted, 'Help, God,' and he did. Within four hours, I was in the care of a wonderful self-help group which started my recovery, and I'm continuing that to this day.

Sean Williams felt intense guilt over his past behaviour, when drunk, to his wife and children, but some of the most moving letters came from listeners who could not forgive themselves for their past behaviour towards their parents.

1 Guilt over Parents

My mum was loving, encouraging and non-judgmental towards me throughout my life. She died aged 72 after a short illness. She became progressively frail and confused—I continued to work, I don't know why, looking after old and infirm people, who were not as needy as she was. What was I afraid of, or blind to? Why couldn't I realise where my priorities should have been?

We nursed her at my sister's home. I quarrelled with my sister in her presence once. I remember feeling so much at odds with everyone and everything. My sisters woke me to be with our Mum when she was dying, and I came with a bad grace and sat at the foot of the bed and just felt angry. Why did she leave me? Now she's gone.

I have two daughters and I try to keep her memory alive by telling them about her, and retelling her stories and songs. I've been through exhaustive psychotherapy, but I cannot come to terms with my guilt. I have no religious faith, but I know how Peter felt when he had denied Jesus three times.

PS I wrote this in the early hours, and now a while later I feel it's self-indulgence to hang onto this guilt for so long, and this intense sadness. I must try to avoid wasting any more time and energy agonising over something which I cannot change.

In this letter, anger and grief are all tied in with guilt. Another listener felt overwhelmed with guilt about his behaviour to his housebound widowed mother, with whom he had lived resentfully for some years in north London before her death. One spring, a few years later, he revisited the place. Out of that, came a poem, from which this is part:

I would come home to you this way
When the evenings were long and bright,
Crossing the road, eager to stay

By an open space looking right
Over a lavish landscape view.
Greatly engrossed in that pleasure,
I did not turn my thoughts to you—
You, I assumed, were at leisure.

Leisure? Sitting by a bare chair,
Walking—if ever—with a frame,
Condemned more than consoled to stare
At television till I came
And had you make my sandwiches,
Grumpily granting you my news:
Blinkered thus to what was vicious?
Blithe? Naïve? Why seek to excuse?

I denied you any powers,
Dictated your last Christmas meal,
Refused you a film star's memoirs,
Made loud radio your ordeal,
And you a captive audience
For my every obsession,
Prattling and ranting with no sense
Of your pain or your oppression ...

... I came back here by the detour
Of years past. Yet I did not pause
This time: that would have been a poor
Return. Others may sing applause
To a beloved landscape scene,
But my praise shall be saved for you—
Though I see you so late: wise, clean
Of heart, selfless, courageous, true.

Whatever happened in the past, I could not believe that the loving parents those two grieving listeners described would have wanted their children to torture themselves with guilt for so long. Kathleen Richardson agreed:

I do believe that where knowledge is, there is forgiveness. With so many of these things, the fault can be on both sides. It's difficult to keep things in perspective when you feel so grieved. It's a vicious circle. You want to do something about it, and you can't, and that makes you feel even more guilty. And once you get into that frame of mind, there's very little that can help.

One thing that *had* helped another listener, grieving after the unexpected death of her sister, was the book *A Grief Observed* by C. S. Lewis. It was as if a voice had spoken to her saying 'Yes, but remember the laughter we enjoyed in years gone by'. She said the guilt had then started to subside.

But Sean Williams commented that many situations have no laughter:

If I look back at my parents, I don't think laughter is something I would associate with them at all. Our house was a house of fear, of pleasing people for the wrong reasons, a house of survival basically; it wasn't a house where laughter had any place at all. But I'm sure if you *can* look back to the good times, then yes, it's obviously cathartic.

Did he ever fear that after his parents' death, he would look back, and think, 'I wish I'd become reconciled to them, when I had the chance'?

I feel hugely guilty about my relationship with my parents. As far as my mother is concerned, for example, I can't hug her, I can't hold her, I can't give her the reassurance that what happened between us is OK—that I've forgiven her, and she's forgiven me. I recognise this in my own kids, particularly the eldest one. There are times when I want to hug her, for the same reasons, I think—I want reassurance from her—and she pulls away, and says, 'Dad, just leave me alone.' I have to let her go, and it hurts like mad, it really does hurt; but I have to accept it. So consequently I feel really guilty about the way, in one sense, I've failed my parents, and I can't deliver what they want, and yet I feel angry because of the situation I find myself in.

Although in very different circumstances, Kathleen Richardson too felt that during her childhood, her parents had loaded her with unnecessarily guilty feelings, when she failed to meet their standards of perfection:

Part of my parents' upbringing of me was to make me fit into their pattern of life, and I was taught a prayer which I said every night of my life until I was about sixteen—I was very late rebelling! The prayer was 'Gentle Jesus, meek and mild, look upon a little child. Pity my simplicity, suffer me to come to thee. God bless Mummy, God bless Daddy, and make Kathleen a good girl.' I think I verily believed, as a child, that the whole thing of religion was designed to make me a good girl, and it really wasn't working.

She says she was constantly told how naughty she was and never given any sense of approval:

I remember coming home from school one day, and running, because I was so proud of myself, and coming to tell my mother that I got 95 per cent in a maths test; and her reaction was 'And what happened to the other five?' I can remember to this day the devastation of not being able to earn approval.

In the last years of her life, her mother had Alzheimer's disease, and the family felt they had lost her:

But in the very last moments before she died, my sister and I were able to look after her, and hold her and comb her hair and wash her; and I think perhaps we were able to repair some of the damage that we felt we'd done to each other.

So Kathleen Richardson was able to resolve some of her complex feelings about guilt and her mother before she died.

3 Guilt over Broken Partnerships or Friendships

I'm presently splitting up with someone I've known for eight years. The man I am leaving still has a lot of feelings for me, but unfortunately I don't have the right feelings for him. I've never really known myself, and I want to be somebody. I hope and feel I'm coming out of the dark tunnel now. I have prayed and feel so guilty because I realise he's hurt, but now, just for now, I'm going to look after myself, not in a selfish way, but I feel that this is the way God wants me to be, just to love me and myself. If anything good has come out of this, it's that we are friends now, and I've learned a lot about what I'm like and how I was in the relationship and how selfish I was.

(Leeds)

I'm a company director. I have my own computer company. Five years ago, I left my first husband for another man. Although I was strong beforehand, once I'd actually left him, I went totally to pieces to the point where I was suicidal. I tried everything, I went to the doctors, I drove the gentleman I ran off with quite crazy over the whole thing, because I was just unapproachable and quite inconsolable over the stress and torment I had caused my first husband. Since coming to terms with my divorce, I've discovered that the true meaning of Christianity is that you can be forgiven, and it has certainly changed my life.

One person who never forgave himself—though in a very different situation—was Judas, who betrayed Jesus:

Jesus then came with his disciples to a place called Gethsemane ... While he was still speaking, Judas, one of the Twelve, appeared; with him was a great crowd armed with swords and cudgels, sent by the chief priests and the elders of the nation. The traitor gave them this sign: 'The one I kiss is your man; seize him'; and stepping forward at once, he said, 'Hail, Rabbi!', and kissed him.
                    Matthew 26.36; 47–50 (NEB)

... Arise, arise, they come, look how they run!
Alas! what haste they make to be undone!
How with their lanterns do they seek the sun!
        Was ever grief like mine?

With clubs and staves they seek me, as a thief,
Who am the Way and Truth, the true relief;
Most true to those, who are my greatest grief:
        Was ever grief like mine?

Judas, dost thou betray me with a kiss?
Canst thou find hell about my lips? and miss
Of life, just at the very gates of life and bliss?
        Was ever grief like mine?
        (from *The Sacrifice*, George Herbert, seventeenth century)

*When Judas the traitor saw that Jesus had been
condemned, he was seized with remorse, and returned the
thirty silver pieces to the chief priests and elders. 'I have
sinned,' he said; 'I have brought an innocent man to his
death.' But they said, 'What is that to us? See to that
yourself.' So he threw the money down in the temple and
left them, and went and hanged himself.*

Matthew 27.3–5 (NEB)

Judas's inability to conceive of any forgiveness seems like his
final betrayal of Christ. Kathleen Richardson thought so too:

I think that must have been one of the deepest sadnesses of
the risen Lord, that Judas wasn't there to receive that forgiveness, and join the disciples in loving, as a result of the
forgiveness they'd received. They were all guilty. One way
and another, none of them had understood and appreciated
what they were doing to him; and yet we see in that lovely
story of Peter, the way Jesus gave him opportunity, having
betrayed him, to speak his love, and to go on to live for
him. That's the joy of forgiveness—it results in wonderful
love.

3 Self-Hatred and Getting through It

One or two letters brimmed over with such guilt they verged on
a self-hatred that seemed to grip like a vice—like this one from a
listener, who with her husband had worked in a form of
Christian ministry. Her husband committed suicide:

**Even now I remember things I had said and done, or not said
and done throughout our married life, and this used to cause
me excruciating mental pain. I used to be very depressed, and
punished myself by not cooking good meals, or spending
money on myself. I even turned the TV off just before the end
of films. After all these years, I am still lacerated by memories
and in my bad moments blame myself for all that has
happened. I find it wise to get up quickly when I wake,
because when lying in bed, the painful thoughts are at their
worst.**

It is because of years of self-torture like this that some New Age and other spiritual teachers challenge some Christian attitudes towards guilt. A story, collected by the Jesuit counsellor, Father Anthony de Mello, puts it this way:

> *The Master was always teaching that guilt is an evil emotion.*
> *'But are we not to hate our sins?' a disciple said one day.*
> *'When you are guilty,' replied the Master, 'it is not your sins you hate but yourself.'*

To Sean Williams, that is absolutely true:

> You just hate yourself, and each time you commit whatever excesses you do, it just drives you deeper and deeper and deeper into the pit. As an alcoholic, you wake up in the morning knowing or not knowing what you've done, and you just feel ashamed and sick of yourself. The only real recourse to dull the pain is to pick up another drink; so you think of another excuse, and off you go. It's not as if you have control over what you're doing—you're almost pro-grammed to do it. Ultimately you hit a point where you just can't stand it, and you either have to go mad, or die, or stop. That's the point I reached on the M6.

Kathleen Richardson says that one of the things that helped her get over her unnecessary childhood guilt was sharing that ex-perience with others:

> And perhaps testing out whether I was right to take all the guilt and blame on myself, knowing that these are things that are shared, and that to carry the full responsibility is inappropriate.
>
> But, having said that, we all do carry responsibility and guilt for some things; and the way often is to test it out. I think sometimes that if we are able just to speak of our own guilt to another, it puts it in balance; and we see we're not really the chief of sinners, that this is something that we can actually speak about to another; and they can still approve of us, and still love us. I think [a stumbling block] is that secrecy, that feeling that if they only knew they wouldn't approve.

That was very much the experience of a listener who said he had been hugely helped by a step-by-step programme at Alcoholics Anonymous. This encouraged him first to seek forgiveness from a higher power (defined by himself; even if only a friend); then to forgive his inner self which the drink had abused; then to forgive those who had harmed him in his earlier life; and finally to ask forgiveness from, and to make amends to, those he had harmed when drinking:

> I have found everybody I've harmed has accepted my amends, with caution, but a genuine desire to help me get over my guilt. AA works because when I tell my guilt, I am talking to a fellow 'expert' in AA, who has been where I was and no longer wishes to be. It's the understanding that God forgives, and that 'normal' people forgive, so forgive oneself.

That is what happened in Sean Williams' self-help group too, though it took him a long time to accept the fact that he could be forgiven—first of all by God, and secondly by any other human being:

> But gradually after a lot of contact with other people in the same situation, I realised that they were in the same boat that I was in, and they'd done things, sometimes—I couldn't believe it—that were actually worse than I had done, which meant that perhaps I wasn't the total renegade, reprobate, I thought I was. That started to give me hope, a forgiveness of myself; and that was really very important. I had to learn to forgive myself. I remember when things got black, I couldn't believe that God actually included forgiveness for me, just because I was something special. But gradually the dawning came that I was included.

The idea of making amends as a way of helping to get over guilt was highlighted by a lighter story from a Cambridge listener, who described herself as 'a classic, well-brought-up, middle-class, public school girl':

> As a girl I had gone to Brownie camp. At the end of the week, we all bought little gifts to take home to our families, and I regret to say I stole quite a number of these to give to my own family. I largely dismissed the incident, and my shoplifting

died out too. But in my early twenties I had a conversion experience and landed up in the Anglican church. In an attempt to clean the slate, and start a new life, one or two of my earlier misdemeanours troubled me. I felt assured of God's forgiveness, but hadn't fully got the whole thing off my back.

I eventually confided in a girl-friend, who firmly and bluntly said, 'Well, there's obviously something you should be doing— what about reparation?' It had never occurred to me that there was anything I could actually do in practical terms to put it right—I didn't know where any of the girls were from whom I'd stolen, and in any case it would be impossible to trace them. However the idea took root, and it just so happened that I had recently met two Brownie pack leaders whose pack very much wanted some musical and percussion-type instruments. Yes, you've guessed it! ... I gather the Brownies are having a lot of fun with the instruments I bought and making quite a racket! I am now genuinely at peace about it.

I know it's a very small and insignificant incident, but seemingly insignificant incidents can take on fearsome proportions. A doctor in charge of a mental home once mentioned to a clergy friend of mine that if he could really assure two-thirds of the people in his care that they were forgiven, they could all go home tomorrow.

A way ahead? or not?
'As long as we don't fall into the trap of buying our forgiveness,' said Kathleen Richardson,

of saying 'I will give back, and that will make God or other people forgive me.' As long as we accept the forgiveness first, and then, because we are forgiven, we want to put things right or do things for other people, I think that's a way. Even if we can't give it back to the person we've harmed, to give it to somebody else is a way of spreading that bit of forgiveness around.

The Lord said to Moses, Say this to the Israelites ... When a man steals an ox or a sheep and slaughters or sells it, he must repay five beasts for the ox and four sheep for the sheep ... When a man burns off a field or a vineyard and lets the fire spread so that it burns another man's field, he must make restitution from his own field according to the yield expected ... When someone gives another silver or chattels for safe keeping, and they are stolen from that man's house, the thief, if apprehended, must restore twofold.

Exodus 20.22; 22.1, 5, 7 (Revised English Bible)

4 Guilt at Failure

Some listeners wrote to describe the guilt of failure, even though they had tried, it seemed, to do their level best:

My son, who's in his early twenties, has been arrested once again. Drugs of all kinds have been his 'siren's song'. For seven years, his brother and I have lived with the misery of the repercussions of David's actions. His father is unable to cope with relationships that cause him any problems, so he's not lived with us for several years.

The last few weeks have been hard to bear. Before Christmas, a woman preacher on the radio talked about the waiting of Mary and all mothers. It was the best Christmas sermon I've heard. It is so hard to wait and dreadfully difficult to know when to support and when to allow a beloved son to carry the full weight of responsibility for his actions. It's such a constant fear that innocent people can be caught up and suffer because of someone that I have brought into the world.

'It's this carrying of responsibility that's so difficult,' said Kathleen Richardson. 'You know each person has to bear some of that themselves, but [the difficulty is] sharing it with other people. I think women particularly are very prone to carry unnecessary burdens.'

A male colleague of mine, the former BBC religious affairs correspondent, Gerry Priestland, suffered for some years from a recurring depressive illness and a sense of guilt and failure. At the time of his depression, the figure of Christ on the cross was of no help to him at all; it only made him feel worse. Christ always seemed to be saying accusingly, 'You did this to me. I am dying in order to pay for your sins.' Behind loomed an angry god, demanding a sacrifice as propitiation. Only later, was he able to jettison his burden of unnecessary guilt and accept God as love.

Kathleen Richardson reminded us what Jesus himself said:

that no one was taking his life from him, but that he was laying it down. He was not a victim. He was a good shepherd laying his life down for the sheep; and that is his gift to us. We didn't steal his life from him.

'Yes,' added Sean Williams. 'In the garden of Gethsemane, Jesus could quite easily have walked away or not been there, or denied what he said; but he just voluntarily, willingly, made the perfect sacrifice of his own free will.'

Love bade me welcome: yet my soul drew back,
    Guilty of dust and sinne.
But quick-ey'd love, observing me grow slack
    From my first entrance in,
Drew nearer to me, sweetly questioning,
    If I lack'd anything.

A guest, I answer'd, worthy to be here:
    Love said, You shall be he.
I, the unkind, ungratefull? Ah my dear,
    I cannot look on thee.
Love took my hand, and smiling did reply,
    Who made the eyes, but I?

Truth Lord, but I have marr'd them: let my shame
    Go where it doth deserve.
And know you not, says Love, who bore the blame?
    My dear, then I will serve.
You must sit down, says Love, and taste my meat:
    So I did sit and eat.

                              (Love III, George Herbert)

One sleepness night, in the dark small hours, I came face to face with the realisation that I had failed utterly in the two things in all the world that meant most to me—my marriage

and bringing up my children. It was so appallingly crushing, I felt I couldn't survive it. For a few moments I knew what hell is like, and then, thank God, the words came into my head 'God can use even failures'. The crushing weight lifted, and I realised that yes indeed, failure in the eyes of the world does not cut one off from God, does not render one useless trash. I've held on to that sentence ever since.

(woman caller, Hitchin)

On a rusty iron throne
Past the furthest star of space
I saw Satan sit alone,
Old and haggard was his face;
For his work was done and he
Rested in eternity.

And to him from out the sun
Came his father and his friend
Saying, now the work is done
Enmity is at an end:
And he guided Satan to
Paradises that he knew.

Gabriel without a frown,
Uriel without a spear,
Raphael came singing down
Welcoming their ancient peer,
And they seated him beside
One who had been crucified.

(The Fullness of Time, *James Stephen*)

Meditation

Come God,
come to the grieving
those who hate themselves,
come to those trapped in the past,
Come and lead us to where you are living
and show us what you want us to do.

Speak, Lord, to our speaking,
Speak, Lord, to our thinking,
Speak, Lord, to our souls' deep understanding.

From the snare of the hunter he will set me free,
He will cover me with his wings
And there I shall find rest and shelter.

Psalm 91.4–5

* * * * * * * *

(Music)

* * * * * * * *

Loving Lord, who grieves over
all the anguish of the world,
give us courage
to face ourselves honestly.
Let us understand who we are
without any pretence,
without being hard on ourselves,
without condemning ourselves,
but with that passion for honesty
that will set us free from the inside out,
and release us to be our true selves.

So, Lord, we lay open to you:
the wounds that have misshaped our lives,
the injuries we cannot forget and have not forgiven.

The wounds *we* have inflicted;
the injuries we cannot forget
and for which we cannot forgive ourselves.

We lay open to you
our thoughtlessness,
not caring of the cost to others,
and all we have left undone ...

our self-hatred,
our self-pity
our wallowing in painful recollections

Lord of our memories,
heal us.

———

Within your circle of healing and peace, we place
Our memories, our guilt,
those whom we have loved and liked ...

those we have betrayed, and abandoned,
those whom we have not liked ...
our enemies ...
those who have died unreconciled to us,
but whom you now reconcile.

And we place in this circle of love and peace
Our families ...
our friends ...
our colleagues ...
all creation.

* * * * * * * *

(Song)

* * * * * * * *

St Julian says:
*Because of our good Lord's tender love to all those who
shall be saved, he quickly comforts them, saying, 'The
cause of all this pain is sin. But all shall be well, and all
shall be well, and all manner of thing shall be well.' These
words were said so kindly and without a hint of blame to
me or to anyone who shall be saved. So how unjust it
would be for me to blame God for allowing my sin, when
he does not blame me for falling into it.*

*In these words, I saw the deep, high mystery of God,
which he will show to us in heaven. Then we shall
understand why he allowed sin to be. And in knowing this,
we shall have a joy in God that never ends.*
        (from Revelations of Divine Love, *fourteenth century)*

* * * * * * * * *

(Music)

* * * * * * * *

(This psalm may be read in turns, taking two verses each, around
a worship circle.)

From the deep places of my soul, I praise you, O God:
I lift up my heart and glorify your holy name ...
From the deep places of my soul I praise you, O God:
how can I forget all your goodness towards me?

You forgive all my sin, you heal all my weakness,
You rescue me from the brink of disaster,
You crown me with mercy and compassion.
You satisfy my being with good things,
so that my youth is renewed like an eagle's ...
... You are full of forgiveness and grace,
endlessly patient, faithful in love.
You do not haunt us with our sins,
nor nurse grievances against us.
You do not repay evil with evil,
for you are greater than our sins.

As vast as the heavens are in comparison with the earth,
so great is your love to those who trust you.
As far as the east is from the west,
so far do you fling our sins from us ...
Just as parents are merciful to their children,
so are you merciful and kind towards us.
For you know how fragile we are,
that we are made of the dust of the earth.
Our days are like the grass,
they bloom like the flowers of the field:
the wind blows over them and they are gone,
and no-one can tell where they stood.

Only your merciful goodness endures ...
... For you have triumphed over the power of death,
and draw us to your presence with songs of joy.
We hear the echo of your angels praising you,
and the whole communion of your saints ...
... From the widest bounds of the universe
to the depths of my very being,
the whispers and cries of joy
vibrate to a shining glory,
O God, our beginning and our end.

(from Psalm 103, Jim Cotter's version)

* * * * * * * *

(Music)

* * * * * * * *

A Rabbi says:
*If anyone has committed a serious sin, let him beware
thinking of it. Let not your soul sink into the mire of sin; it
may not be able to extricate itself and repent ... Turn away
from evil; hold it not in remembrance; do good. If you
have sinned much, balance it by doing much good.
Resolve today, from the depth of your heart and in a joyful
mood, to abstain from sin and do good.*

The prophet Jeremiah says:
   Listen to the words of the Lord ... Mend your ways and
your doings'. Deal fairly with one another, do not oppress
the alien, the orphan, and the widow, shed no innocent
blood in this place, do not run after other gods to your
own ruin. Then will I let you live in this place, in the land
which I gave long ago to your forefathers for all time.
                              Jeremiah 7.2, 5-8 (NEB)

May Holy Wisdom
kind to humanity,
steadfast, sure and free,
the breath of the power of God;
may she who makes all things new, in every age,
enter our souls,
and make us friends of God,
now and always. Amen.

                         (St Hilda Community)

                    (Music)

                    * * * * * * *

Some Suggestions for Worship Music

1 'Reverie' from *Deux Arabesques* by Debussy.
2 *String Quartet in A Minor, op. 132*, by Beethoven.
3 Hymn: 'Just as I am' (Tune: Saffron Walden).
4 'O Be Joyful in the Lord' by John Rutter, from CD *Te Deum*
(OUP/Collegium Records).

Other Music

6 'Regrets' sung by Andy Williams, from single *Regrets*
(Chappell Music/CBS).
7 *Introduction and Allegro* by Ravel.
8 *Piheno* by Bartok.
9 *St Luke Passion* by Penderecki.

Acknowledgements

The most important thanks go to all those who wrote or phoned in with their stories, and also the studio guests, who contributed so much, and had the courage to risk being so honest on air. Without them, this book would have been impossible.

Over the last twenty years, with BBC religious broadcasting colleagues, I have shared what feels like several hundred emotions (delight, stress, fury, disappointment, fear, amusement, love, grief, exhaustion, etc, etc). Special affectionate thanks to producers Claire Campbell Smith, Canon Noel Vincent, Clair Jaquiss, Dr Bert Tosh, Mo McCullough and Shirley Scott.

Extracts from the Authorised King James Version of the Bible, which is crown copyright in perpetuity in the United Kingdom, are reproduced by permission of the Crown's patentee, Cambridge University Press.

Extracts from the *New English Bible* © 1961, 1970 Oxford and Cambridge University Presses.

Extracts from the New International Version of the Bible © 1973, 1978, 1984 by the International Bible Society. Published by Hodder and Stoughton.

Extracts from the *Good News Bible (Today's English Version)* published by the Bible Society and Collins, © American Bible Society 1976.

Extracts from the *Revised English Bible* published by Oxford University Press and Cambridge University Press 1989.

Extracts from prayers by the St Hilda Community, Monica Furlong, David Adam and Janet Morley, are reproduced by permission of SPCK (books listed in bibliography).

Material from the Wild Goose Worship group is © WGRG, Iona Community, Glasgow, Scotland.

Thanks too to Father Denis Blackledge, SJ, whose 'Loving Lord' prayers provided the basis for a number of prayers in the meditations.

Also to the Reverend Jim Cotter for permission to reproduce his versions of the psalms.

Extract from *Anger's Freeing Power,* from *The Collected Poems of Stevie Smith* (Penguin Twentieth Century Classics) is reproduced by permission of James MacGibbon.

The quotation from Bertolt Brecht's *The Threepenny Opera,* translated by John Willett and Ralph Mannheim, published by Methuen London, is reproduced with the permission of Reed Consumer Books.

Thanks to Gujarat Sahitya Prakash, Anand, India, for the stories collected and retold by Father Anthony de Mello, SJ. The Master in his stories is not a single person. He is a Hindu Guru, a Zen Roshi, a Taoist Sage, a Jewish Rabbi, a Christian Monk, a Sufi Mystic. He lives in the seventh century BC and the twentieth century AD.

Permission to quote from Anthony de Mello's *The Heart of the Enlightened* is given by HarperCollins Publishers Ltd.

James Stephen's poem *The Fullness of Time* is reproduced by permission of the Society of Authors, on behalf of the copyright holder, Mrs Iris Wise.

Extracts from *The Teaching of Buddha* published by Bukkyo Dendo Kyokai (Buddhist Promoting Foundation, Tokyo, Japan).

If, through difficulty in tracing copyright holders, a copyright holder has not been credited, please contact the publishers and due acknowledgement will be made in subsequent editions.

Further Reading

Worship

Appleton, G., ed., *The Oxford Book of Prayer*. Oxford 1985.
Blackledge, D., *Loving Lord Horizons*. Sanctuary Books 1992.
Cotter, J., *Healing—More or Less: Reflections and Prayers at the End of an Age*. Cairns 1990.
Cotter, J., *Pleasure, Pain and Passion: Some Perspectives on Sexuality and Spirituality*. Cairns 1993.
Cotter, J., *Prayer in the Morning: A Book for Day's Beginning*. Cairns 1989.
Cotter, J., *Prayer at Night: A Book for the Darkness*. Cairns 1991.
Cotter, J., *Through Desert Places: A Version of Psalms 1–50*. Cairns 1989.
Cotter, J., *By Stony Paths: A Version of Psalms 51–100*. Cairns 1991.
Cotter, J., *Towards the City: A Version of Psalms 101–150*. Cairns 1993.
Cotter, J. and Pelz, P., *Prayer in the Day: A Book of Mysteries*. Cairns 1992.
Julian of Norwich, *Revelations of Divine Love*. Penguin 1978.
Morley, J., *All Desires Known*. SPCK 1992.
Morley, J., ed., *Bread of Tomorrow: Praying with the World's Poor*. SPCK/Christian Aid 1992.
Morley, J., *Companions of God: Praying for Peace in the Holy Land*. Christian Aid 1994.
Stuart, E., *Daring to Speak Love's Name: A Gay and Lesbian Prayer Book*. Hamish Hamilton 1992.
The St Hilda Community, *Women Included*. SPCK 1992.
Van de Weyer, R., ed., *The Fount Book of Prayer*. HarperCollins 1993.
Wild Goose Worship Group, *A Wee Worship Book*. Wild Goose 1989.

The Poems of George Herbert. Oxford 1941.
Praise in All Our Days: Worship from Taizé. Mowbray 1983.
Praying with John Donne and George Herbert. Triangle 1991.
With All God's People: The New Ecumenical Prayer Cycle. WCC Publications 1990.

Poetry

Eliot, T. S., *Collected Poems 1909–1962.* Faber 1963.
Smith, S., *Selected Poems.* Penguin 1978.

Anthologies

Adam, D., Borderlands: *The Best of David Adam.* SPCK 1991.
Armstrong, K., ed., *Tongues of Fire: An Anthology of Poetic and Religious Experience.* Penguin 1987.
Causley, C., compiler, *The Sun Dancing: Christian Verse.* Puffin 1982.
De Mello, A., *The Heart of the Enlightened.* Fount 1989.
De Mello, A., *One Minute Nonsense.* Gujarat Sahitya Prakash 1992.
De Mello, A., *The Song of the Bird.* Gujarat Sahitya Prakash 1989.
De Mello, A., *Taking Flight: A Book of Meditations.* Image 1988.
Dwyer, S., ed., *Playing with Fire: A Natural Selection of Religious Poetry.* Villa Books 1980.
Enright, D. J., ed., *The Oxford Book of Death.* Oxford 1987.
Every, G., Harries, R., and Ware, K., eds., *Seasons of the Spirit.* SPCK 1984.
Gollancz, V., *A Year of Grace: Passages Chosen and Arranged to Express a Mood about God and Man.* Gollancz 1950.
Greene, B., and Gollancz, V., collectors and arrangers, *God of a Hundred Names: Prayers and Meditations from Many Cultures.* Gollancz 1985.
McEachran, F., *A Cauldron of Spells.* Greenbank Press 1992.
Peale, N. V., ed., *Courage and Confidence.* Cedar 1993.
Van de Weyer, R., *Celtic Fire: An Anthology of Celtic Christian Literature.* DLT 1990.
Whittaker, A., ed., *All the End Is Harvest: An Anthology for Those Who Grieve.* DLT/Cruse 1984.

Others

Adam, D., *The Eye of the Eagle: Meditations on the Hymn 'Be Thou My Vision'.* Triangle 1990.
Beckett, W., *Art and the Sacred.* Rider 1992.
Blackstone, J., and Josipovic, Z., *Zen for Beginners.* Writers and Readers 1986.
Blue, L., *Day Trips to Eternity.* DLT 1987.
Bonhoeffer, D., *Letters and Papers from Prison.* SCM Press 1971.
Cragg, K., *The Wisdom of the Sufis.* Sheldon 1976.
De Mello, A., *Sadhana—A Way to God: Christian Exercises in Eastern Form.* Image 1978.
Herrigel, E., *Zen in the Art of Archery.* Arkana 1985.
Lewis, C. S., *A Grief Observed.* Faber 1961.
Parrinder, G., *The Wisdom of the Early Buddhists.* Sheldon 1977.
Roberts, M. V., *Dreamtime Heritage: Australian Aboriginal Myths.* Rigby 1975.
Stryk, L., and Ikemoto, T., trs. and selectors, *Zen: Poems, Prayers, Sermons, Anecdotes, Interviews.* Swallow Press/Ohio University Press 1981.
The Oxford Bible Reader's Pocket Concordance. Oxford 1984.
The Teaching of Buddha. Bukkyo Dendo Kyokai 1985.